Animal Rights – A Question of Conscience

ISSUES FOR THE NINETIES

Volume 3

Editor

Craig Donnellan

Independence
Educational Publishers
Cambridge

First published by Independence
PO Box 295
Cambridge CB1 3XP

British Library Cataloguing in Publication Data
Animal Rights – A Question of Conscience (Issues for the Nineties Series)
I. Donnellan, Craig II. Series
179.3

ISBN 1 86168 010 4

Printed in Great Britain
City Print Ltd,
Milton Keynes

Typeset by
Claire Boyd

Cover
The illustration on the front cover is by
Katherine Fleming / Folio Collective.

CONTENTS

Chapter One: Animal Experiments

Chapter Two: Blood Sports

Introduction

Animal Rights – A Question of Conscience is the third volume in the series: **Issues For The Nineties**. The aim of this series is to offer up-to-date information about important issues in our world.

Animal Rights – A Question of Conscience looks at animal experiments and animal sports.

The information comes from a wide variety of sources and includes:
Government reports and statistics
Newspaper reports and features
Magazine articles and surveys
Literature from lobby groups
and charitable organisations.

It is hoped that, as you read about the many aspects of the issues explored in this book, you will critically evaluate the information presented. It is important that you decide whether you are being presented with facts or opinions. Does the writer give a biased or an unbiased report? If an opinion is being expressed, do you agree with the writer?

Animal Rights – A Question of Conscience offers a useful starting-point for those who need convenient access to information about the many issues involved. However, it is only a starting-point. At the back of the book is a list of organisations which you may want to contact for further information.

*****

Is animal research justified?

Using animals for medical research is an issue which arouses strong feelings, and which has polarised public debate for many years. Here we bring you a range of views

A question of balance

All major medical research charities in the UK believe that animal research is justified – on balance. Once all the conflicting tensions are taken into account, charities that belong to the Research for Health Charities Group (RHCG) are sure that the benefits outweigh the costs.

The medical charities only use animals where there is no other suitable research technique; and only then when the work is important enough to justify their use. Within the RHCG we work together, sharing information about animal welfare, and the advances made in non-animal techniques, and are all committed to minimising any possible suffering.

There is no simple right or wrong view about the use of animals. Our society eats animals and their products, wears them, uses them for entertainment, and kills some species, such as rats and mice, as vermin. In this context, in a society which uses animals in all these different ways, it is ethical to use animals in medical research to understand, prevent, treat or cure disease. But even this strong statement needs qualification, since most people agree that it is wrong to use animals without proper care and consideration, or thoughtlessly or pointlessly.

Many medical advances rely heavily upon animal work, such as the development of insulin for people with diabetes, transplants, blood transfusions, anaesthetics and vaccines. To claim otherwise is to rewrite history. Although all modern medicine rests in part on animal studies, its major work is on cell and tissue culture, computer models, studies of healthy human volunteers,

hospital patients in clinical trials, and the analysis of large populations.

Only 2-3% of medical charity research funds are spent on animals, their food, care and welfare, and the vets and technicians to look after them. Even though the direct cost of the animals is small, around 20% of all projects will involve an element of animal studies in amongst the other research techniques. Ultimately our overall understanding of diseases rests heavily upon studies of living systems, including animals. In the fight to save lives, animals are vital.

Myc Riggulsford, Director,
Research for Health
Charities Group

Animal welfare is key

Experiments on animals cause them various degrees of suffering – due to the experiments or their effects, or

the distress of confinement in laboratory cages. In law, such suffering is justified by the benefits experiments are said to bring. In diabetes research the benefits are described broadly as the understanding, prevention or treatment of diabetes. There is thus a conflict between human and animal interests which presents a serious ethical dilemma for individuals or organisations concerned with the welfare of either, or both.

The RSPCA's objectives are to promote kindness and prevent cruelty to animals. The Society is opposed to all experiments which cause pain, suffering or distress, and thus resolving the conflict of human/animal interests is a major concern. Our ultimate goal is to see animal experiments replaced with humane alternatives. The reduction of animal use and animal suffering is an

immediate objective. It can be achieved by scrutinising the need for every project and each animal used, and by ensuring suffering is avoided – but this depends on sufficient commitment from all concerned.

As substantial funders of research, medical charities are ideally placed to influence animal welfare within the scientific community. They should look at projects they fund and plan to fund in future and ask: is the research essential or are there alternative approaches? Must animals be used to achieve the research goals? Do the potential benefits to humans outweigh the costs to animals? And all completed projects should be reviewed retrospectively to ensure that their aims were met, otherwise animal lives have been wasted. The public contribute substantially to medical charities but are concerned about animal as well as human suffering and their concern merits more than the standard response that 'animals are only used when absolutely necessary'. Necessity is in any case a subjective judgement.

Where animal use is considered unavoidable, medical charities should ensure high standards of animal welfare are set. Individual charities could set up a task force to identify where most suffering occurs in the work they fund and investigate ways of mitigating this.

Grants should only be awarded on condition that research establishments meet certain ethical and welfare criteria. This could have a major impact on reducing the burden on animals that research imposes. It is not easy, but the animals deserve no less.

Maggy Jennings, Head of Research Animals Department, RSPCA

Does it work?
Were it not for the protection of the Animals (Scientific Procedures) Act 1986, most, if not all, scientists who use animals would at one time or another have appeared in a court of law on a charge of 'cruelty to animals'.

No wonder, for in the name of progress and medical knowledge scientists have induced heart attacks, peptic ulcers, paralysis and epileptic seizures in animals, forced them to

smoke cigarettes, drink alcohol, ingest heroin, and used them as living targets of military weapons and in germ and chemical warfare.

In the search to discover new medicines, chemicals are tested for effect on animal 'models' of human diseases. These models are conditions in animals which are supposed to resemble a human illness. They are usually created artificially by surgery or by dietary, hormonal or chemical treatment, and sometimes by breeding animals with a particular susceptibility to the disease. Unfortunately, not only can these experiments cause pain, distress and suffering: they are often scientifically inadequate.

A new drug is tested for safety on as many as 1,000 animals. Apart from the problem of different species (and even different strains of the same species) responding differently to drugs, factors such as temperature, humidity, the time of day an experiment is conducted, the food and handling animals receive, and the type of bedding used all affect the outcome of an experiment. So animal tests do not rule out the possibility of side-effects; studies with healthy volunteers and patients (clinical trials) still provide the first reliable indication of the effectiveness and safety of new drugs.

The objects of Advocates for Animals are 'the protection of

animals from cruelty, the prevention of the infliction of suffering, and the abolition of vivisection'. Although we hold strong views on animal research, we accept that the alternative techniques to replace all animal experiments are not yet developed and believe that no one has the right to criticise, for example, people suffering from a particular condition as they cling to the hope of a cure and getting better through animal research.

Animal experimentation is a genuine dilemma. It is wrong to allow people to suffer and die if that suffering and death can be prevented by, say, drugs, vaccination or surgery. However, Advocates for Animals believes that it is also wrong if this involves the imprisonment, pain, suffering, and death of countless millions of sentient creatures. We therefore believe that science and the animal welfare movement has a moral duty to work together to right this wrong as soon as possible.

Les Ward, Director, Advocates for Animals

Increasing our understanding
There's public perception that all people with diabetes need to do is take insulin and that's the end of the problem. Of course, for many people with diabetes, whether they take insulin or not, the other part of the equation is complications, including nerve damage. So how can animal experiments contribute to our understanding of diabetic complications?

If we can understand the consequences of high blood glucose levels, we can develop new drug therapies to reduce the risk or slow the development of complications. Although people and rats appear to be very different, the similarities in basic biochemistry are reflected in many aspects of the changes diabetes causes. For example, in both rats and humans, the blood flow that is crucial to the survival of nerves is reduced, and diabetic rats also develop the early stages of complications. But surgical procedures are needed to measure blood flow, which means that it's inappropriate to conduct routine screening of potential therapeutic drugs in humans. Nor can blood flow be studied in cell culture, which is sometimes seen as an alternative to animals. Experiments in laboratory rats have revealed complex interactions between some of the mechanisms that control blood flow through nerves and we are beginning to understand how and why this changes with diabetes. In certain promising cases, doses of drugs that only have a small effect on their own show a considerable effect when combined. Of course, such new drug combinations still need to be tested in clinical trials, and these are currently being planned.

Researchers are bound by the requirements of legislation governing the care of laboratory animals. Rats live under '5 star' conditions, with clean bedding every day, as much food and water as they want, and a vet on call. We should bear in mind that, in the UK, for every rat used in medical research ten are exterminated as pests.

Dr Mary Cotter, researcher

Using our knowledge well
Turning a scientific theory into a new medicine is a long, complex process. Pharmaceutical companies need to use a variety of research methods, depending on the questions that have to be considered at each stage. Though we would all wish it were otherwise, some of this research must currently be done in animals.

Animal research is essential to study those effects of potential new medicines which cannot be seen using computers and test-tubes. Medicines ultimately have to be studied in people but only after scientists and doctors feel confident they can do so without undue risk. However much we care about animals, human health and safety come first.

But non-animal methods are making a difference. Advances in our understanding of the behaviour of different chemical structures, along with new technology, have led to a whole new field of computer design.

Increasing knowledge about how specific cells live and function has made it possible to study the effects of a potential new medicine on cells, tissues and organs in the test-tube. Only those compounds which look promising will go on for further study. As a result, most compounds will be eliminated before animal studies begin.

Computer and test-tube studies are important parts of the research process, but the information they give is still limited. This is because many of the potential effects of medicines occur as a result of long chains of biological events which we cannot simulate on computer or replicate in a test-tube. Most of these complex effects can, however, be seen in studies with laboratory animals.

The biological similarities between ourselves and other animals are enormous. There are, of course, species differences that always have to be considered. But animal research gives necessary guidance about the likely effects of a medicine in people. Without this research, testing medicines in people would expose them to a level of risk our society could not accept.

No amount of testing can guarantee the safety or effectiveness of a medicine for every single person. Scientists do the best they can, using the most up-to-date scientific knowledge and a combination of the most appropriate research methods, to bring safe and effective treatments to patients.

As our biological knowledge increases, the usefulness of non-animal methods will also increase. In the meantime, organisations under whose auspices animal research is conducted have a moral and legal obligation to follow the principles and ensure the practice of good laboratory animal welfare.

Marjorie Johnson,
Animals in Medicines Research
Information Centre
● The above article appeared in the October/December 1996 issue of *Balance.*

© British Diabetic Association

Uses of animals in research and testing 1994

In 1994, 19% of procedures were carried out for legislative purposes; 13% under medical legislation and 6% for legislation concerning other kinds of products.

Purpose	Number	Approx % of total	
Development of medical/ dental products and appliances –			
Toxicity tests	268,300	(9.4)	
Non-toxicity tests	788,986	(27.8)	37.2
Development of veterinary products and applicants –			
Toxicity tests	24,667	(0.9)	
Non-toxicity tests	89,665	(3.2)	4.1
Fundamental studies of body structure and function	700,066		24.6
Production/maintenance of sera, tumours and infectious agents	361,509		12.7
Safety evaluation	217,225		7.6
Breeding for genetic defects	256,516		9.0
Miscellaneous uses, diagnosis, surgical techniques, education/training	135,427		4.8
Total procedures 1994	2,842,361		

Source: RSPCA

Campaigning to end animal experiments

The British Union for the Abolition of Vivisection (BUAV)

Towards the end of the last century, public opposition to animal experiments began to rise sharply. It was against this background that philosopher and social reformer Frances Power Cobbe founded the British Union for the Abolition of Vivisection (BUAV) in 1898. Today, nearly 100 years later, the BUAV still leads the campaign to end animal experiments.

The early campaigners spoke eloquently of the need to end vivisection, but social and technological changes have meant that in the late twentieth century we are able to campaign far more effectively on behalf of suffering animals.

Nowadays, we use an increasingly sophisticated approach to the problem. We are able to employ such methods as computer searches and undercover investigations to expose the often secret world of animal testing. The power of the media is then used to ensure that our findings are made public. By harnessing the support which press stories generate we can apply pressure on commercial concerns to stop them using animals in experiments.

One place where we have always ensured that animals have had a voice is in Parliament, although our lobbyists are now equally at home in Brussels and Strasburg as they are in Westminster. Our political profile is now at an all-time high and we enjoy the support of MPs from all major parties. Such support is vital, as without it we will never be able to achieve the changes in the law necessary to save animals from the horrors of the laboratory.

To make sure our arguments are heard and understood, the BUAV produces a wide selection of educational materials. These range from specialist publications such as the parliamentary briefing sent to all

MPs to the hundreds of thousands of information packs we send to our supporters and members of the public. Such educational materials are backed up with campaign videos, books and exhibitions.

But some things have changed little over the years. Just as we did in 1898, we continue to stimulate debate about the moral and scientific issues involved in animal experimentation. And whether it be in television or radio studios; the church hall or the town hall; the boardroom or the classroom, BUAV representatives can be heard speaking on behalf of suffering animals.

The BUAV in action

The BUAV has undertaken many ambitious campaigns and investigations in recent years which have not only gained widespread media attention and public support, but have resulted in real victories against animal suffering.

For instance, our undercover investigators were able to reveal that a dog 'dealer' was supplying retired racing greyhounds, intended for family homes, to laboratories. Widespread media coverage resulted in the closure of the dealer's business and the introduction of tighter rules by the National Greyhound Racing Club.

A massive investigation into the international trade in primates for research revealed evidence of shocking cruelty to animals. As a result we have launched a worldwide campaign to end this appalling trade. Early on in the campaign, it was discovered that two well-known wildlife parks were supplying monkeys to British laboratories. After the press covered our story, both parks immediately stopped the practice.

We also led the UK campaign which managed to stop car manufacturer General Motors using animals in crash tests – a major victory against one of the world's largest companies.

Our 'Choose Cruelty-Free' campaign began on a high note when clothing giant Benetton was persuaded to drop all animal tests for their cosmetics range. Since then the campaign, backed by many well-known celebrities, has gone from strength to strength with a whole host of cosmetics companies abandoning animal testing. Many major companies such as Sainsbury's and Co-op actually sought our advice before implementing a 'cruelty-free' policy.

Every time our investigators work undercover in laboratories we gain more evidence that animal experiments are cruel and unnecessary. We can also show how even the woefully inadequate laws which are meant to give laboratory animals some protection are not being enforced. Recently the Home Office was forced to take strong action after we discovered that unnecessary animal use and falsification of test data were taking place at a major British testing centre.

By bringing the shocking truth of animal experiments to the attention of the public and Government, each new BUAV campaign and investigation brings the end of animal experiments one step closer.

What is vivisection?

'Vivisection' literally means 'the cutting up of living animals'. But the term is now used generally to describe a variety of experiments which are carried out on over three million animals each year.

Toxicity tests are routinely performed on dogs, rabbits, rats and mice by commercial companies. Animals are given often huge doses of substances by injection or force feeding and then observed for symptoms such as convulsions, vomiting, breathing difficulties and cries of pain. Anything from drugs to insecticides can be tested in this way.

Products such as weedkillers and cosmetics are used on animals in irritancy tests. The most notorious of these is the Draize test where substances are dropped into the eyes of rabbits.

Thousands of animals are subjected to barbaric treatment during psychology experiments. Methods used in experimental psychology include starvation, separation of young animals from their mothers, electric-shock treatment and deliberate brain damage.

The growth of genetic engineering has made a big impact on the vivisection industry. Now experimenters can ensure that animals are 'programmed' from birth to develop painful and deadly diseases, so that they can be used as mere laboratory tools.

These examples represent just a few of the many ways animals can be made to suffer in laboratories. Experiments are conducted by profit-seeking companies, medical research charities, universities, hospitals and public health organisations.

Why is vivisection wrong?

The BUAV was founded on the philosophy that inflicting pain, suffering and death on helpless animals during experiments is morally wrong. And for many the moral argument is sufficient reason to oppose vivisection.

But there is also a wealth of evidence to show that animal experiments are misleading and divert attention and resources away from more fruitful avenues of research.

The notion that results from animal tests can be directly applied to humans has been proved false time and time again:

- Aspirin causes birth defects in cats but not in humans
- Penicillin is toxic to guinea pigs and hamsters
- Morphine sedates people but excites cats
- Benzene causes leukaemia in humans but not in mice
- Saccharin causes cancer in rats but not in humans

There is always a real danger that, because of our reliance on animal tests, unsafe drugs and other products can be released into the market-place for human use. An example of this was the heart drug Eraldin. Although their drug was thoroughly tested on animals, it had devastating side-effects on human patients – including blindness and even death – before it was withdrawn from the market.

Many members of the scientific community agree with our views on animal testing.

'. . . The knowledge gained from studies in animals is often not pertinent to human beings, will almost certainly be inadequate, and may even be misleading.'

Arnold D. Welch,
Department of Pharmacology,
Yale University School of
Medicine

'. . . The sad reflection must be that the countless animals who have died in psychology experiments have died not only cruelly, but in vain.'

Don Bannister,
Medical Research Council
External Scientific Staff,
High Royds Hospital

There are many alternatives to animal experimentation. Some of these methods, such as population and clinical studies, have been used successfully for years and some methods have been developed recently with advances in scanning and computer technology.

A great deal of research can be conducted in test-tubes using human tissue cultures which have proved to be an extremely effective means of developing drugs and producing vaccines.

Unfortunately, research to develop non-animal testing methods is seriously underfunded. To try and alleviate this problem the BUAV is calling for a Government-funded strategy to promote the use and development of humane research methods.

Animal testing causes needless pain and suffering to thousands of animals each day. It is of little or no value and can, in fact, produce dangerously misleading results. Relying on animal testing drains time and resources away from the use and development of more valuable research methods. Humane and superior research alternatives do exist. For these reasons, the BUAV is campaigning to end animal testing and stop the suffering of animals.

© BUAV

Information about animal research

Many people have strong feelings about the use of animals for medical research. Heated and emotional debates are common. But what are the facts? Sensible discussions are difficult without clear, factual information. This article gives the facts and figures, using information from medical publications and official reports.

Why are animals used in experiments?

There are six main areas of medicine and biology where animal experiments need to be used:

Developing new treatments for diseases

To conquer disease a lot of work is put into developing better medicines and surgical operations as well as making vaccines and finding other ways of preventing diseases. Much of this work is for human medicine. Some is to treat diseases suffered by both humans and animals. Some is specially for animal medicine. Polio and diphtheria vaccines, insulin for diabetes, and kidney transplants are all examples of medical advances that depended on animal research. This sort of research will be needed for the new medicines and other treatments of the future. There are many diseases that we cannot yet cure. Examples are multiple sclerosis and certain cancers, as well as new diseases like AIDS. For these, and for other conditions, animal research plays an essential part in the search for cures.

Fundamental biological and medical research

Fundamental (or basic) research in medicine and biology is done to find out more about what keeps humans and animals alive and healthy. When we understand how the body works when it is healthy we can then find out what goes wrong when disease strikes. Animal research has been vital for discoveries such as how kidneys work, or how hormones control different parts of the body. Today, basic research in many areas of biology and medicine still needs animal experiments. A good example is the brain: there is still a lot we do not know about how it works. If we are to find an answer to this important question, fundamental research needs to continue. Fundamental research is to medicine as the foundations are to a house: if you haven't dug the foundations properly then the house will either fall down or be impossible to build in the first place.

Preparing nature products used in medical research and treatment

Animals can produce useful medical substances in their blood or milk. These antibodies, vaccines or hormones are important for diagnostic tests, medical treatments, and basic research. One day we may be able to make more of these substances artificially. At present many of them have to be produced using animals.

Safety testing

We use many different chemicals every day. These chemicals turn up as medicines or household products, as well as in manufacturing, or as fertilisers and pesticides used for farming. These chemicals must be tested to make sure that they are as safe as possible for animals and people. Safety testing is done to guard against products which could cause cancer or birth defects, or could harm the environment. This is vital for the health of both people and animals as well as showing a proper concern for the environment.

Studying genetic diseases

There are many diseases that are inherited or partially inherited – these are caused by faults in a person's

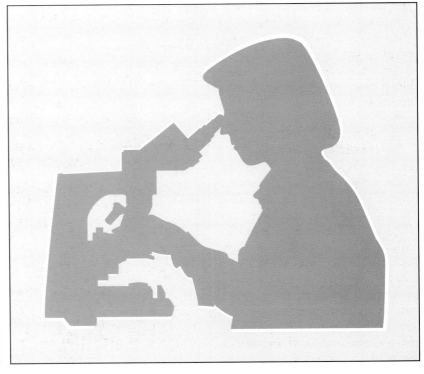

genetic code. Some of these genetic diseases are fatal, like Duchenne muscular dystrophy, which is caused solely by having faulty genes. Some long-term illnesses such as diabetes or rheumatoid arthritis probably have a combination of causes. Faulty genes, infection, poor diet and other unknown factors are all thought to play a part in causing these conditions.

Sometimes animals have exactly the same genetic fault that humans do. For example, there is a kind of mouse which naturally develops muscular dystrophy, because it has the same faulty gene as human muscular dystrophy patients. This animal plays a vital role in research into that illness. Scientists can now alter genes and breed strains of mice or other animals with particular genetic diseases. This may lead to treatments for sickle-cell disease and other inherited or partially inherited diseases. Breeding rodents with cystic fibrosis has already helped researchers to develop promising new treatments for this condition.

Development of new methods to diagnose diseases

Diseases need to be diagnosed as accurately and as quickly as possible if the best treatment is to be given. Animal experiments have been vital in improving diagnosis. Diagnostic methods include scanning to check on the health of unborn babies, to identify some cancers, or to diagnose heart disease. Animal research has also led to many blood tests for the diagnosis of infectious diseases.

How much animal research is done?

In Great Britain, there were just over two and three-quarter million scientific procedures using animals in 1994. The exact figure was 2,842,361. The actual number of animals used was a bit less than this, as some animals were used more than once. This is allowed sometimes so that animals' lives are not wasted, but it is very strictly controlled. To put this figure into context, about 700 million animals are used to provide food every year

in Britain. A reasonable estimate is that about 8 million animals are destroyed as vermin and as unwanted pets.

The number of animal experiments done each year in this country has fallen by about 3 million over the last 20 years. This is due to higher standards of laboratory animal welfare and stricter controls

---

Scientific procedures using animals range from mild to substantial. A mild procedure would be something like a change of diet or environment, giving an injection or taking a small blood sample. Examples of moderate procedures include some testing of potential medicines and most surgery under general anaesthetic. Major surgery would be classified as substantial. Most procedures are mild. Only a small proportion of procedures are of substantial severity.

The number of animal experiments done each year in this country has fallen by about 3 million over the last 20 years. This is due to higher standards of laboratory animal welfare and stricter controls. The drop can be uneven – for example, in 1991 and again in 1994, there was a tiny rise in the number of procedures – but the overall trend is probably still downwards.

Table 1: Major advances in basic research that depended on animal experiments

1600s	Discovery of blood circulation Discovery of the function of the lungs
1700s	Measurement of blood pressure
1800s	Vaccination to stimulate immunity Understanding of infectious diseases
1900s	Discovery of antibodies Understanding of hormone systems
1920s	Discovery of vitamins
1930s	Discovery of the mechanism of nerve impulses Discovery of tumour viruses
1940s	Understanding of embryonic development
1950s	Understanding of the control of muscle activity Understanding of energy metabolism Understanding the mechanism of hearing
1960s	Discovery of monoclonal antibodies Understanding the biochemical functions of the liver
1970s	Understanding of transplantation antigens Understanding the way the brain functions Discovery of prostaglandins
1980s	Development of transgenic animals Understanding the basis of memory
1990s	Understanding of the genetic basis of atheroma (furring up of arteries and veins) Importance of nitric oxide (NO) as a local acting chemical messenger

Table 2: Major medical advances which depended on animal research

1900s	Corneal transplants
1920s	Insulin for diabetes
1930s	Modern anaesthetics for surgery Diphtheria vaccine
1940s	Broad-spectrum antibiotics for infections Whooping cough vaccine Heart-lung machine for open-heart surgery
1950s	Kidney transplants Cardiac pacemakers and replacement heart valves Polio vaccine Drugs for high blood pressure Development of new materials and surgical techniques for joint replacements Drugs to treat mental illness
1960s	Rubella vaccine Coronary bypass operations Heart transplants
1970s	Drugs to treat ulcers Improved sutures and other surgical techniques Drugs to treat asthma Drugs to treat leukaemia
1980s	Immunosuppressant drugs for organ transplants CAT scanning for improved diagnosis Life-support systems for premature babies Drugs to treat viral disease
1990s	Genetic therapy for cystic fibrosis Electronic implants for treatment of deafness and paralysis

What medical advances have come from animal research?

Medical research in the last 100 years has produced many ways to treat and prevent diseases. Table 1 lists some of the main discoveries in basic research which relied on animal experiments. The development of many major medical treatments has also depended on animal research. Table 2 lists some better-known examples of these. Without research on animals it is unlikely that any of these would have been discovered.

Why are there special controls on animal research?

Research on animals, like some other medical areas (such as test-tube babies or organ transplants), can pose tough moral questions. Without such research, many modern medical treatments would not exist. We would not have the treatments which save the lives of both people and animals and prevent much suffering. There is every reason to believe that future medical advances will continue to depend on animal research. The same is true for veterinary medicine.

Some animal experiments could involve distress and pain and we have a duty to limit this as much as possible. People in Great Britain have been concerned about animal welfare for over 100 years. Since 1876 there have been special controls on the use of experimental animals. These controls were revised and extended as the Animals (Scientific Procedures) Act 1986. This law permits important medical research and testing, but ensures that any animal distress is kept to a minimum. It goes further than most other European controls on animal research. The laws and regulations governing animal experiments in Britain are widely accepted as the strictest in the world.

How is research on animals controlled?

The Animals (Scientific Procedures) Act 1986 requires that, before a researcher can use animals, he or she must have special licences. These licences are granted by the Home Secretary.

Such licences are granted only if:

- The potential results of the research are important enough to justify the use of animals.
- The research cannot be done using non-animal methods.
- The minimum number of animals will be used.
- Dogs, cats and primates are only used when it is absolutely necessary.
- Any discomfort or pain is minimised by the appropriate use of anaesthetics or painkillers.
- The researchers conducting the experiments have the necessary skill, training and experience with laboratory animals.
- The research laboratory has the necessary facilities to care for the animals properly.

The law says that animals must be examined every day and that a vet must be on call at all times. Any animal judged to be in any pain or distress which cannot be relieved must be immediately and painlessly killed. To enforce the Act the Home Office employs a team of inspectors who have to be qualified vets or medical doctors. These people ensure that all animal-based research is done strictly according to these controls.

Sources of information:
Statistics of Scientific Procedures on Living Animals, Great Britain 1994, HMSO; *Guidance on the Operation of the Animals (Scientific Procedures) Act 1986*, HMSO;
An Outline History of Medicine, Phillip Rhodes, 1985, Butterworths; *Man and Mouse*, Professor William Paton, 2nd edition, 1993, Oxford University Press.

© *Biomedical Research Education Trust, 1996*

Why do we use animals for research?

Is it because:
a) They are less intelligent than us?
b) They feel pain less than us?
c) Their lives are not as important as ours?
d) They are weaker than us?
e) We have traditionally used them and it has become acceptable?
f) There is no other way for progress?

Let us consider each question in turn.

a) We use animals because they are less intelligent than us.

Most animals are classed as less 'intelligent' than humans, but what exactly is meant by this expression? By 'less intelligent' do we mean they cannot speak, or that they cannot stand up for themselves, or even think? True, animals cannot speak, and neither can they defend themselves against man, but this does not mean they cannot think. Neither does any of this diminish their ability to suffer pain and distress. If we are going to classify creatures by how intelligent we think they are, then this is a form of discrimination that could easily be applied to humans – and no one would accept that.

b) They feel less pain than we do.

We can never know how much pain another person feels, we can only imagine it because we know what it feels like to be in pain ourselves. Similarly, we can never know how much pain an animal feels, but we can imagine it. Most higher animals have a nervous system similar to our own. If we consider the prerequisites for pain are a central nervous system connected to pain receptors, there is no reason at all to suppose animals feel any less pain than we do. Indeed, on the basis of this, most scientists use animals for pain research because their pain is like ours. Besides, animals show when they are in pain – if you kick a dog it will yelp; if you insert tubes into the brains of conscious rats they will feel pain.

c) We use animals because their lives are not as important as ours.

Feeling on this subject may very much depending on religious views, or feelings about life in general. For those who see humans as the centre of the universe with everything at their disposal for their convenience, then animals will merely be there to eat, wear, and use at their will. This attitude is called 'speciesism'. On the other hand, it can be argued that all life is equally valuable and should be treated with respect. It must be remembered though, that experiments are carried out on live animals and the level of suffering must be taken into account as well as the importance of life itself.

d) We use animals in research because they are weaker than us.

If we cause suffering to animals in laboratories because they are weaker than we are, we are acting in a disgraceful way – like bullies attacking someone smaller than themselves. There have been times in the past when people were experimented on because they were powerless and the perpetrators of this were eventually punished. So how is what we are doing to animals any different?

e) We use animals because we have traditionally used them.

Things that have always been are often taken for granted, but this does not necessarily mean they are right. The slave trade, inhumane as it is was, was acceptable to many people because things had always been that way. Progress and changes for the better only happen when people start thinking differently. Indeed, looking back, scientific evidence seems to suggest that animal testing has hindered the progress of medical research.

f) We use animals because there is no other way.

There are other ways – and better ones too! The Humane Research Trust believes that non-animal medical research is not only more humane, but more reliable too. After all, what would you prefer – taking medicine that has been tested on a mouse, or taking medicine that has been tested on human cells just like your own?

The moral issues

Today we accept that all humans should have equal rights whatever their colour or sex. We use words like 'racism' or 'sexism' to describe attitudes that are unfair to certain groups. We believe that how we treat people should not depend on the country of their birth, nor on whether they are a man or woman, but on the fact that they are all people and deserve to be treated with equal consideration.

We say all this because people have rights. This means it is important to each person what happens to them. We do not want to be hungry or cold, frightened or hurt because these things cause us to suffer. Animals also have rights. They do not choose to suffer either and they too should be treated with equal consideration. A lack of concern for other creatures simply because they are of a different species is called 'speciesism'.

Animals do not need the same rights as us. A puppy does not need to vote and a cat does not need the right to a good education, but all animals are entitled to the right not to suffer. Scientists accept that animals feel pain just the way we do, so do we have the right to make animals suffer? Man is an animal too – just a different species.

The Revd Andrew Linzey in his book *Christianity and the Rights of Animals* condemns all experiments – whether on animals, criminals or embryos. He believes people justify them on the basis of benefit – the benefit of one creature at the expense of another. This philosophy inevitably justifies other evils and if our thinking is dominated by this utilitarian attitude, then there is 'no right, value or good which cannot be bargained away'.

'I believe if you can find it in your heart and mind to empathise with and respect non-human life, then I think your capacity, your capability, for love is that much greater. Joining this movement is like "loving thy neighbour" in its highest sense.' Donald Barnes – American National Anti-Vivisection Society.

Medical and non-medical experiments

Many people feel that animals must suffer if the end result is better for people, but they object to animals being used in laboratories for other reasons. For example, it may be considered wrong to use an animal to test a new lipstick or shampoo, but if it is to try and develop a new drug that may save lives, then that might be considered a good enough reason to use animals. But before you decide, consider the following:

1) Does an animal suffer any more or less whether it is a weed-killer, a cosmetic or a medicine that is being tested?

2) Since there are alternatives that are practical, effective and safer, would it not make sense and be more civilised to use those instead of animals? Those who oppose us (such as scientists who use animals or breeders who sell animals) often accuse us of caring more for animals than people, but this is nonsense. Those committed to animal welfare are equally committed to human welfare.

3) Many medical experiments carried out on animals are because people damage their own health, either through a bad diet, smoking or drinking too much, not taking proper exercise. Should animals suffer because we allow ourselves to become ill through bad habits?

4) There are already thousands of medicines available in this country. For some minor illnesses such as headaches and coughs, there are already many preparations on the market. Do we really need so many medicines?

5) When a pharmaceutical company brings a new drug on to the market, they can patent it for many years. This means no other firm is allowed to make and sell that particular drug. The other firms want to make money by selling that kind of drug, so they produce one almost the same but with a slightly different formula. These are called 'me too' drugs. Should medicines be produced just to make a profit for the firms that manufacture them?

Are medicines always the best thing for our health? We all hear stories of being addicted to drugs, of terrible side effects, along with many cases of over treatment and bad treatment. Is taking drugs the answer?

● The above is an extract from *Alternatives to animals*, a schools pack published by the Humane Research Trust. See page 39 for address details.
© The Humane Research Trust

Vermin or life-saver?

It depends on your point of view

If you saw a wild mouse or rat in your house, you would probably want to get rid of it. You would regard it as vermin, a word used to describe a great variety of unwanted, troublesome or dangerous animals. But the close cousins of these intruders, the laboratory mice and rats used in medical research, help save lives.

Most major medical advances have depended on laboratory animals. These advances include vaccines for infections such as polio and for animal illnesses such as canine distemper and feline enteritis; safe anaesthetics for modern surgery; medicines to control diabetes, asthma and high blood pressure; and life-support systems for premature babies. We have probably all benefited from this research. Millions of lives have been saved.

Medical research using animals must continue. Although great progress has been made, there are still all too many serious illnesses that doctors cannot cure or treat effectively. We want cures for cancer and a vaccine for AIDS. We want to help the children affected by fatal genetic disorders like cystic fibrosis and muscular dystrophy. We want to stop the suffering caused by arthritis, Alzheimer's disease and Parkinson's disease.

Why are animals used in research?

Animals are used in research because they are biologically similar to human beings. All mammals, including humans, have the same organs – heart, lungs, kidneys, liver etc. – performing the same functions. This similarity explains why many veterinary medicines are the same, or nearly the same, as medicines for human patients.

There are stages in most research programmes when it is not enough to know how individual molecules, cells or tissues behave. In the living body these parts interact in very complicated ways which we need to understand.

So there are limits to test-tube and computer-based research. There are also limits, both scientific and ethical, to the experiments that we can do using people. The alternative is to use a suitable animal. This may be necessary during the basic study of healthy systems or during research into a disease. It is essential during the development of a new medicine, alongside testing in the test-tube and testing on healthy volunteers and patients.

Are there alternatives?

No one would use animals in research if it wasn't necessary. Those involved in research care about animals just like anyone else, and funds are too scarce to waste on unnecessary research. For these reasons, and because there are very strict controls, animals are used humanely and only when there is no alternative. A lot of effort goes into trying to reduce the numbers of animals used, and trying to develop new methods to replace animals. As a result, the number of laboratory animals used annually in this country has almost halved in the last 20 years.

Non-animal methods – tissue culture, computer modelling, studies of patients and populations – are widely used. In fact, only about 5p in every £1 spent on medical research goes on animal studies. The word alternatives is often used to describe non-animal methods. This can lead to confusion because these methods are generally used alongside animal studies, not instead of them. All these techniques have their place, and it is rarely possible to substitute one for another.

As science progresses, it may be possible to reduce the numbers of animals used in some areas. In other areas, the numbers of animals may increase. For instance, new and better animal models may be developed. It is now possible to breed animals with exactly the same genetic faults that cause some human diseases. So mice with cystic fibrosis, for example, have the same symptoms as children with cystic fibrosis. These mice are the ideal way to test gene therapy, which may offer a medical breakthrough for the disease.

Are the animals well looked after?

The British controls, laid down in the Animals (Scientific Procedures) Act, are widely regarded as the best in the world. They set high welfare standards for laboratory animals. Research animals are kept in clean conditions, well fed and looked after properly by experienced carers. It is important to make sure they are treated humanely and do not suffer from stress or carry unwanted diseases. They are usually specially bred for research. About 8 in 10 laboratory animals are mice or rats.

Most experiments do not cause much pain or distress, since they involve only mild procedures such as a simple injection, taking a small blood sample, or a change of diet. In most of the rest, anaesthetics and painkillers are used to prevent discomfort, just as they would be for a human patient.

Putting the numbers in context

- Over 600 million animals are consumed annually as meat in the UK. This is more than 200 times the number of animals used in research.

- The average person in this country will consume, in a 75-year life span, 600 chickens, 20 sheep, 22 pigs and 4 cows. On behalf of the same person, medical research will use about 3 mice and 1 rat.

- There are probably about 8 million rats and mice killed as vermin every year in the UK. In 1992, official figures show that 2.26 million purpose-bred rats and mice were used in medical research and testing.

- 2 million pet cats and dogs are abandoned every year, many of these having to be put down by welfare organisations such as the RSPCA. About 12,000 cats and dogs are used annually in research – about the same as the number of pets abandoned every 2 or 3 days. All cats and dogs used in medical research are specially bred.

• The above is an extract from a leaflet called *Vermin or life-saver?*, published by the Research Defence Society. See page 39 for address details.

© *Research Defence Society*

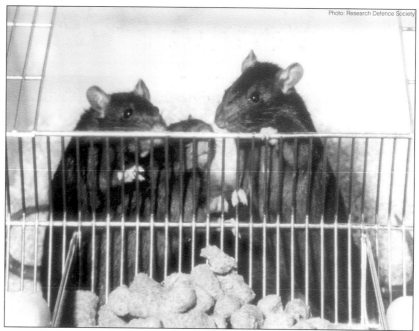

Photo: Research Defence Society

Rodents are used in 85% of animal procedures

Alternatives to animal experiments

RSPCA information

What is an alternative?

An alternative is anything that can be used instead of a live animal in a scientific experiment. Cells grown in test-tubes (cell cultures) are a good example, so are organs taken from animals killed for other reasons. Computers and videos are also useful, especially for teaching.

Why are animals used instead of alternatives?

The reason animals are used in experiments is that certain scientific questions can only be answered using whole living bodies. Humans cannot be used in experiments that would harm them, so animals are used as substitutes or 'models' for humans or other animals. In this way scientists study how the body works and why it goes wrong. The research may lead to the development of new treatments for human and animal diseases, although it does not always have this aim in view. Animals are also used to test the safety of new medicines and of chemicals used in homes, farms and factories.

Some parts of this work can be done without animals. But diseases affect whole living bodies, and it is whole living bodies which react to medicines and chemicals. Because bodies are so complex, it is not always possible to get all the answers about them from tests on simple cell cultures. Of course animals and humans are not exactly the same but the results of experiments on animals are used to try to predict what may happen in humans or other animals.

Why can't human volunteers be used?

Humans are not allowed to be used in experiments if there is any serious risk to their health or life. They are used after the animal-testing stage in the development of medicines, and human volunteers do test some

cosmetics, but again only if there is thought to be no serious risk to their health.

Can alternatives always be used?

Many people believe that there are alternatives to all the animal experiments that are carried out at the moment. Unfortunately this is not true and more research is needed to develop more replacements for animals. In many cases, the only 'alternative' that avoids using animals is not to do the experiment. This always spares animals. Whether it matters or not to humans depends on the aim of the research, i.e. whether it is to develop a new household product or an AIDS vaccine.

So when are alternatives used?

Most research to develop alternatives has taken place in toxicity testing – where animals are used to see if products are harmful to humans or the environment. The first stages of

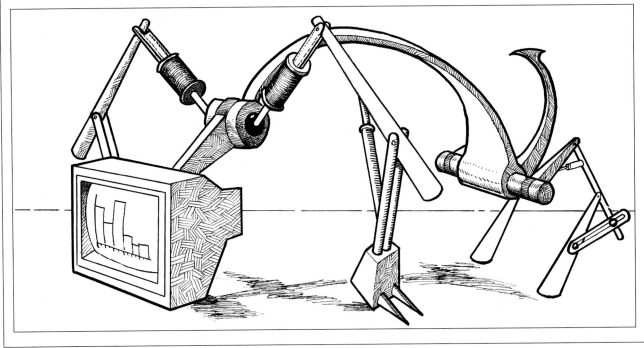

testing can usually be done on cell cultures. This means that very harmful products are not tested on animals. Many researchers are working on alternatives to the Draize eye test (in which rabbits are used to find out if substances will cause eye irritation) and to some types of skin tests.

Some medicines can be designed using computers, although animals are still used to see how well they work and whether they are safe to give to humans. All vaccines for people are now made without using animals, although animals are still used to check their safety. Computers and videos are being used more and more for teaching in schools, colleges and universities.

Even when there are no complete replacements, alternatives may be used at some stages of research or the direction of the research may be changed to reduce or avoid animal use.

What problems must be solved before alternatives can replace animals?

In many cases, the use of animals for research and testing is required by regulations or the law. To replace animals in these tests three things have to be done:

- An alternative technique has to be invented – one that gives the same or better information than the animal test does.
- The technique has to be validated (shown to work reliably in different laboratories).
- Lastly it has to be approved by the people that make our laws.

Unfortunately this can take many years.

What can we do in the meantime?

Where alternatives do not yet exist or are not possible, the RSPCA places great emphasis on the need to refine the way that experiments are carried out to make them more humane so that animals suffer as little pain and distress as possible. Staff of the RSPCA's Research Animals Department work with the many scientists concerned about animal welfare to make the changes the Society wants to see.

The RSPCA's view

The RSPCA believes that much more time and money should be spent by the Government and industry on looking for alternatives to animal experiments. It is also very important that this work is co-ordinated effectively so that no time is wasted in replacing animals as soon as possible, wherever possible.

The RSPCA also believes that much more time and money must be spent on finding ways to prevent pain and suffering in those animals that are still used. The actual need and justification for each individual experiment and each individual animal used must be looked at more closely. This is very important.

The Society is working very hard to convince the people with authority in science, industry and government that both the replacement of animals in experiments and the refinement of experiments to minimise suffering are priority issues. Implementation of both must be speeded up.

You don't have to dissect

Waste of life

Thousands of animals – like mice, rats and frogs – are bred and killed so they can be dissected in school biology lessons. Methods of killing include a violent blow to the back of the head and suffocation. Dissection encourages us to see animals as 'objects' – to be used and then discarded when it suits us. It teaches us to ignore the rights of animals. But now many young people reject this outdated attitude. They think it is time for schools to stop this pointless slaughter.

If you agree, say 'no' to dissection!

Waste of time

A look at the gory insides of a pregnant rat is hardly essential to your education. You don't need to cut up eyeballs, hearts and other organs from dead farm animals or fish either.

In fact dissection is not necessary for biology exams . . . so there's no reason for it to be included in coursework.

In schools, human biology is taught by using diagrams, videos and models . . .not by dissecting dead humans! Animal biology can be taught in the same way.

Examining boards

Examining boards no longer require dissection for practical exams or for assessed coursework – at GCSE and at A-level. This breakthrough was a result of campaigns opposing dissection and the actions of school pupils who refused to dissect. You can help ensure that animal dissection is removed from the biology syllabus altogether.

Remember, you don't have to dissect

Your right to refuse

If you object to this needless cruelty you have the right to refuse to carry out or watch dissection. Discuss your views with your teacher and ask to be given an alternative assignment.

Refusing to dissect is not about being 'squeamish', it's about having respect for animals.

Action

- Refuse to dissect.
- Send for our petition which calls for an end to dissection in schools.
- Send for more leaflets to give to your friends.

'Animal research helped save my daughter's life'

You always think, it'll never be my daughter; it'll never happen to me . . . I'll never forget that day. The doctor told me that only 100 people in the country had this condition. If left untreated, Maria's liver would have been destroyed. He said there was medicine we could give her . . . I didn't think of anything except saving my daughter . . . No one can understand what it's like, until you go through it yourself.'

Maria is not alone – millions of men, women and children owe their lives to medical research involving animals. Without it, the possibility of finding successful treatments for serious diseases would be dramatically reduced.

Animals in medical research – a doctor writes

Professor John Martin, British Heart Foundation Professor of Cardio-vascular Science, writes:

'It is vitally important for children like Maria, and adults too, that animal research continues. Medical research, much of which depends on animals, will help us discover what leads to conditions such as Maria's liver disease, and find

Immunisation against infectious diseases, such as polio, diphtheria, TB and meningitis, has been developed through animal research. UNICEF says that immunisation saves the lives of over 3 million children every year

Information from

RDS

out how to treat patients. And the more we can understand a disease, the more likely it is that we may be able to prevent it.'

Medical research methods
'There are many methods used in research into diseases. We can use computers, cells and tissues in test-tubes, and study patients in hospitals, as well as studying animals. In fact, all the non-animal methods are very widely used, because animals are only used in research when absolutely necessary. However, at some stage we need to study the effects of a disease, and ways of treating it, on a whole living animal. It is not ethical to carry out such experiments on people, so the only alternative is to study an animal which has the same, or a very similar, disease.'

Research on heart disease
'I deal with heart-attack patients. I often see middle-aged patients (usually men) die of this disease. So fathers are removed from their families, bringing much unhappiness and hardship. We know that the disease that causes heart attacks is hardening of the arteries. This process, which can kill a patient at 50, may have started at 30. So in patients we can only see the final stages of a process which has been going on for a very long time.

'Badly damaged arteries do not give us enough information about how the disease process started and developed. We know some of the factors involved in heart disease, such as cigarette smoking and high-cholesterol food. We can educate people in the hope that they will avoid these. But this is not the whole story, because the biggest cause of death in people with *low cholesterol* levels is still a heart attack. There must be many causes that we still do not know about.

'We can study the first things that go wrong in a human artery by following the process from the beginning in animals. The animals

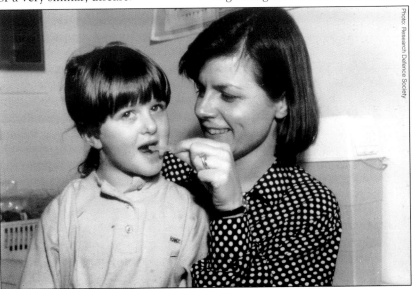

Photo: Research Defence Society

we use have very similar blood systems. By understanding this process in animals we can aim to prevent suffering and death from heart disease.'

Why do we need to do research?
'Stopping animal research would severely handicap medical progress in many key areas. Some might argue that we've learnt a lot already, so why don't we stop, and just use the drugs we have? We may have learnt a lot, but there is even more that we don't yet know.

'Hundreds of thousands of people are still disabled or killed by heart disease in this country every year. It is worth remembering that, although it may now be possible to reduce the risk of coronary heart disease, the causes are complicated, and family history is just as important as other factors. And many heart conditions are completely unconnected with lifestyle. What about the 5,000 children born every year with congenital heart defects?

'Heart disease is not the only area where medical research is still needed. In this country one in every five people dies from cancer, often with great suffering. Thousands of children suffer and even die from inherited diseases. We don't have all the answers. If we were to stop using animals in medical research, I can't see how we could get those answers.

'You really have to ask yourself, although we value animals very much, do we value them more than people? Perhaps some people do, but I believe that people must come first. I also believe that all the medical advances that we have achieved so far justify the use of animals in medical research.'

Laboratory animal welfare
'Every animal experiment must be carefully considered beforehand:
- Could it be done some other way without animals?
- Could it be done with fewer animals?
- Is it designed to be as humane as possible? – and, most of all –
- Is the research important enough to justify using animals in the first place?

A few people in the UK who benefited last year from medical research involving animals

300
heart transplants

4,000
artificial heart valves fitted

15,000
had coronary bypass surgery

180,000
diabetics kept alive with insulin

3,000,000
operations under general or local anaesthetics

30,000,000
prescriptions for asthma

50,000,000
prescriptions for antibiotics

Without animal research, the possibility of finding better treatments for serious diseases such as cancer, AIDS and multiple sclerosis would be dramatically reduced. Animal research saves lives

Sources:
UK Transplant Support Service Authority
Compendium of Health Statistics 1992, Office of Health Economics
Cardiac Surgical Register, Society of Cardiothoracic Surgeons
Diabetes in the UK 1988, British Diabetic Association
© *Research Defence Society*

'Only when all these questions have been answered would you decide to involve animals in your research.

'Like other medical researchers, I try to avoid any suffering for our animals. During medical experiments we treat them very much as we would treat our patients. We give them drugs to relieve pain and, for operations, we use a sterile operating theatre and a proper anaesthetic. In this country all animal research is carried out under very strict laws and monitored closely by the Home Office. Every research project involving animals must have a licence. Home Office Inspectors, who are all doctors or vets, make sure that the welfare of laboratory animals is safeguarded.'

The future
'Maria and her family know that animal research helped save her life. For the last four years she has taken medicines which stop her liver from failing. Medical research involving animals is important in trying to understand what has caused Maria's liver disease, and to develop better treatments or even a cure. In future, better understanding may lead to ways of preventing this and other deadly diseases. For the sake of patients and their families, animal research must continue.'
● The Research Defence Society is an organisation of doctors, vets and medical researchers which informs the public about the role of animals in medical research
© *Research Defence Society*

Animals in research

The facts about animal experiments

Every year in this country under the Animals (Scientific Procedures) Act 1986 over 3 million experiments are performed on animals. Many of these experiments involve pain, suffering and distress and are carried out whilst the animal is fully conscious. According to official Home Office statistics these animals can be subjected to experiments involving burning, scalding, blinding, electric shocks, exposure to irradiation, interference with the central nervous system and many other procedures intended to produce pain.

Much emotional play is made on the need to use animals in medical research, but information is now suggesting that many animal experiments are invalid and serve to confuse rather than enlighten. Drugs are tested on animals but the side-effects are often not exhibited in the animal models. Despite increased animal testing the incidence of side-effects in the human population continues to rise. The incidence of cancer also continues to rise because animal models often give false positives/negatives when used to test potential cancer agents. Similarly in the fight against AIDS, despite numerous attempts to induce this disease in animals (particularly chimpanzees), no animal has developed AIDS. It remains a uniquely human disease.

Apart from the use of animals in medical research many tens of thousands of animals are used each year in the testing of new unnecessary, inessential products such as beauty preparations, weed-killers, pesticides etc. by a test known as the LD 50 test (the lethal dose that kills 50% of the animals under test) which the research industry itself considers of doubtful value. Indeed, some researchers have gone so far as to call it useless.

Advocates for Animals

What scientists say about animal experimentation

'Countless animals have been surgically dismembered, drugged, starved, fatigued, frozen, electrically shocked, infected, cross-bred, maddened and killed in the belief that their behaviour, closely observed, would cast light on the nature of human kind.'

(Dr Don Bannister, Medical Research Council External Staff, *Animals in Research*, published by John Wiley and Sons.)

'Over 7,000 animals were subjected to procedures that induced distress, despair, anxiety, general psychological devastation or even death. The results of this research have had little impact on clinical practice, and the potential for future advances seems limited. Many experiments were trivial extensions of past research, or simply were attempts to reproduce in animals what was already known about humans.'

(Dr Martin L Stephens, *Maternal Deprivation Experiments in Psychology: A Critique of Animal Models*.)

'I believe the scientific community does not have too much time left in which to demonstrate its bona fides. We are all aware of continuing abuses of animals which should have stopped years ago.'

(Dr R. W. Gee, Director of the Australian Agricultural Health and Quarantine Services – *Proceedings of Animal Experimentation Seminar on Ethical, Scientific and Legal Perspectives*.)

'Scientists have re-written medical history, grossly exaggerating the role of animal research in biomedical progress.'

(Dr Stephen Kaufman, *Medical Research Modernisation Committee Report*, Vol. 2, No. 1.)

What scientists say about laboratory animal housing

'The majority of captive primates live in pathogenic conditions which are either preventable or reversible and therefore indefensible.'

(Dr William McGrew, University of Stirling, *Int Stud Anim Prob* 2(1).)

'When you have spent 27 years of your life with wild, free chimps and come to know them as individuals, to appreciate them as beings with whom we share this planet, of course it is horrifying to see them shut into tiny cages. Chimpanzee infants have the same emotional needs and expectations as human infants. To imprison pairs of three-year-old chimpanzees in cages that are 22 inches by 22 inches and two feet high is just as inhumane, just as cruel, as it would be to imprison human toddlers in tiny cages. To incarcerate young chimps in total isolation, with nothing to do, no friendly contact with other living beings – other than short utilitarian visits by caretakers – is to drive them to insanity. It is hard for me to understand how anyone, with access to the knowledge about chimp mentality that exists today, can treat them in that way.'

(Dr Jane Goodall (referring to laboratory in the USA).)

'Many laboratories in Britain that house live animals for experiments fail to keep them in satisfactory conditions.'

(Dr Gerald Clough, Environmental Consultant.)

Invalidity

'Many scientists were experimenting on vast numbers of animals without rhyme or reason. The animals were being injected with huge doses of drugs or chemicals which were totally unnecessary. Up to 90% of these results are discarded because they are not applicable to man.'

(Professor Dennis Park, University of Surrey and Advisor to The World Health Organisation, speaking at a Humane Research Trust Conference.)

'Infecting the chimpanzee has very little value. If you want to follow the progress of this disease (AIDS) there are sufficient humans already infected. And is what goes on in a chimp's body relevant to what goes on in a human today?'

(Dr Richard Tedder, Consultant Virologist at Middlesex Hospital.)

'In spite of repeated injections of tissues from infected patients, no chimpanzee has ever developed AIDS. AIDS remains a uniquely human disease.'

(Physicians Committee for Responsible Medicine, PCRM Update.)

'Killing millions of rodents in mass screening experiments has failed to produce a single new and effective human chemotherapeutic agent that had not been previously discovered clinically. Even worse than this fiasco is the fact that quantitative extrapolation from animals to man gives false or misleading results that have caused much unnecessary suffering and death among human cancer patients.'

(Dr Irwin D Bross, President, Biomedical Metatechnology, Inc *Medical Research Modernisation Committee Report*, Vol. 2, No. 3.)

© *Advocates for Animals*

The alternative to animal testing

Information from the Fund for the Replacement of Animals in Medical Experiments (FRAME)

A problem of conscience

Every year, around 100 million experiments are performed on living animals throughout the world, nearly 3 million of them in UK laboratories. The effects can be truly horrifying – such as severe damage to the eyes or brain, or slow poisoning to death.

Scientists justify the need for this type of experimentation as essential to their quest to understand and conquer disease. Indeed, if medical research is to continue, if new drugs are to be developed and if the remaining diseases which threaten the quality of human and animal life are to be overcome, animal experiments cannot simply be halted overnight.

New chemicals and valuable consumer products must be adequately assessed to safeguard those likely to be exposed to them, and to protect the environment as a whole. However, many of the routine animal toxicity tests conducted for these purposes, despite causing much pain and distress, actually provide little or no useful information at all.

Various laws demand animal testing, but this type of experiment is increasingly unacceptable, not only to members of the general public, but also to many scientists.

This suffering cannot be allowed to continue . . . and FRAME is working scientifically and logically to bring it to an end

The way forward

Better design of medical experiments and the rationalisation of toxicity testing is already reducing the number of animals used.

Where some experiments involving animals can still be justified, the procedures used are being refined – to minimise any pain, distress or suffering caused.

However, the ultimate goal of FRAME is the total elimination of the need for any experiments on living animals – through the development and use of relevant and reliable replacement methods.

What is FRAME doing?

Research programme
Working in collaboration with universities, polytechnics and industrial companies in the UK, Europe and North America, FRAME sponsors and conducts research into alternative techniques and their use in toxicity testing.

Scientific validation
In order for alternative tests to be accepted, they must first be shown to be relevant and reliable. FRAME is working with others in a unique series of validation programmes, to help accelerate the acceptance of non-animal techniques.

Data bank
The use of animal tests is now illegal

if the results sought can be obtained by using other means. INVITTOX, the unique data bank developed by FRAME, provides scientists throughout the work with up-to-date information on alternative methods for use in toxicology.

Toxicity committee
FRAME co-ordinates a committee of expert industrial and academic scientists who are assessing the prospects for reducing and replacing animal procedures in all areas of routine toxicity testing.

European and parliamentary liaison
FRAME maintains regular contact with more than 100 Members of Parliament through the All-Party Parliamentary FRAME Group and acts as a consultant to the Commission of the European Communities and various European governments in relation to the development and management of validation schemes and the application of alternative techniques.

Education
By providing balanced and inform-

ative educational material, together with visiting speakers, FRAME encourages teachers, students and schoolchildren to discuss the ethics of animal experimentation and the potential use of alternatives.

Publicity
Regular appearances in the press and on radio and television ensure promotion of FRAME's logical approach to bringing about an end to animal experimentation.

© FRAME

Animal research and the development of a new medicine

Summary
Turning a scientific theory into a new medicine now takes, on average, 12 years. During that time, computer models of new molecules will be studied, thousands of variations will be investigated in the test-tube and a small number will go on to be studied in animals. Then, if doctors and scientists are confident they can do so without undue risk, the potential new medicine will be studied in people.

Animal research is essential to help scientists evaluate the safety and effectiveness of new medicines. This is because most of those effects of a new medicine which are not yet predictable by using computer models or test-tube research can be seen in well-designed and conducted animal studies.

The biological similarities between ourselves and other animals are enormous. Animal research therefore provides essential guidance enabling researchers to bridge the gap between the test-tube and the patient. There are, of course, species differences between ourselves and other animals but, compared to the similarities, the differences are minor and are always considered.

Animal research is not a cheap option and is conducted under strict UK legislative controls.

Unexpected effects
Even after years of intensive study, and a comprehensive evaluation of all the data by both the originating company and the Government's licensing authority, medicines sometimes cause unexpected side-effects in general use. Those who campaign against animal research frequently cite such side-effects as an argument against animal testing but this is to misunderstand the careful step-by-step nature of the research process.

No one expects animal studies to provide all the necessary information and final decisions are never made on the basis of animal tests alone. Rather, they enable researchers to move as close as possible to the human situation, before a new medicine is tested and used in people. All medicines approved since the introduction of the Medicines Act 1968, including ones later found to have unexpected effects, passed all the testing stages including non-animal, animal and human research.

No amount of testing can guarantee to find all possible side-effects for every person who may take

Scientific procedures involving animals			
Mouse	51.9%	Other carnivore	0.1%
Rat	26.6%	Primate	0.2%
Other rodent	5.0%	Other mammal	1.3%
Rabbit	2.4%	Bird	6.7%
Cat	0.1%	Reptile/amphibian	0.6%
Dog	0.3%	Fish	4.9%

Total approximately 2.8 million procedures

8% of the procedures were for non-medical safety testing (based on Home Office figures for 1994)

a medicine. A reaction which occurs at a rate of 1 in 100,000 people or even at a lower rate of 1 in 10,000, for instance, may not be seen until very large numbers of people use the medicine.

Do computers help?

Computers have made research much more efficient and have therefore helped to reduce the number of animals needed. Computers have been particularly important in the design of potential new medicines, where existing knowledge is used to 'design in' features that could be helpful and 'design out' features likely to cause harm.

But however advanced technology has become, biological knowledge is still limited and computer modelling only makes theoretical molecules. This is a long way from testing a real medicine in the living body. As knowledge of our biology increases, so too will the contribution computers make to medicines research.

Can cell culture be used more?

Cell-culture work in the test-tube is used wherever possible and its usefulness will continue to increase as knowledge improves of how our cells work in the body. This is desirable not only for humane reasons but also because today's cell-culture work is much cheaper and faster than the animal tests it replaced.

Cell cultures do not, however, tell us about the range of effects (both helpful and harmful) which only occur when a medicine is in the complete living body, as opposed to cells in isolation.

How is animal research regulated?

The Animals (Scientific Procedures) Act 1986 aims to strike a balance between the needs of research and the welfare of laboratory animals.

The main requirements of the Animals (Scientific Procedures) Act 1986 are that:
- Only competent people can conduct the research;
- Research premises must have the staff and facilities to look after the animals properly before, during and after procedures;
- The likely benefits of the research must justify any possible distress to the animals.

The law also aims to ensure that studies are well designed so that as few animals as possible are needed and requires that non-animal alternatives are used wherever applicable. Where animals are needed, appropriate steps must be taken to ensure that any distress they may experience is kept to the minimum possible given the nature of the research. Proper veterinary care must be provided at all times.

Most laboratory animals experience no, little or only momentary pain, but, where more pain is likely, researchers must plan in advance how they will prevent or relieve it.

Home Office approval of each research project must be granted before the work can begin and their inspectors regularly visit laboratories, often unannounced, to check that the Act's requirements are being followed.

Will the number of animals needed be reduced?

The overall trend is downward. The number of procedures involving animals has nearly halved in the last 20 years even though the overall amount of medicines research during the same period has increased.

However, the amount and type of animal research conducted varies from year to year as new possibilities to treat hitherto untreatable illnesses arise and specific health or safety concerns come to light.

Is the pharmaceutical industry committed to animal welfare?

The UK pharmaceutical industry fully recognises its responsibility to obey the spirit as well as the letter of the law. The ABPI believes that all organisations under whose auspices research is conducted must ensure that they create a culture which embodies the principles and encourages the day-to-day practice of good animal welfare. The UK pharmaceutical industry has a well-deserved reputation for high standards of laboratory-animal welfare.

The ABPI is also taking a major role in international discussions between the pharmaceutical industry of the US, the EU and Japan, along with their respective medicines regulatory authorities, to ensure that those tests demanded by governments around the world are consistent so that duplication or unnecessary animal research is eliminated.

© *The Association of the British Pharmaceutical Industry*

Cosmetics and product testing

Every year thousands of animals suffer misery, pain and death in experiments to test cosmetics and household products such as soap, shampoo, deodorant, hair dye, toothpaste, sunscreen and lipstick, paints, bleaches, glues, polishes and washing powders.

In fact most of the products that are sold in the high-street shops have been tested on animals.

Why are cosmetics and other products tested on animals?

At present, the law does not specifically require cosmetics to be tested on animals, only that companies ensure the safety of their products. This enables cruelty-free companies to develop and market their ranges without animal experiments. European guidelines, however, recommend that companies perform animal experiments before they market newly developed ingredients, so animals are still used by some manufacturers. Recently it was agreed that cosmetics testing on animals throughout Europe should end by 1998, but only if alternative test methods were deemed acceptable.

What sorts of tests are performed?

Toxicity (poisoning) test

The test substance is added to food or water, or is force-fed to the unfortunate animal through a long syringe directly into its stomach. After they have been dosed with the substance, the animals are observed for any symptoms of poisoning, such as tremors, bleeding, vomiting or loss of balance. The test may last for many days and any animals that do not die of poisoning during the experiments are killed at the end and autopsied.

Skin irritancy test

This test involves shaving and scratching a patch of a guinea pig or rabbit's skin before applying the test substance. The animals are often held in a restraining device to stop them licking or rubbing the test area. Again they are observed for signs of irritation such as reddening, swelling, cracking, bleeding or ulceration of the skin. The test lasts for several days and no pain relief is given.

Eye irritancy test

In the Draize test a substance is dripped into the eyes of rabbits to see if it causes any irritation or damage. During the test, which lasts for several days, the unfortunate animals are held in stocks to stop them wiping or rubbing their eyes. They are given no pain relief. Rabbits are used because they have large eyes and because they have poor tear ducts which means they can't wash away the test substance. This test pro-

cedure, like all the others, can cause great suffering to the animals.

The nonsense of it all is that these cruel tests don't work – they don't make products any safer. Many experts are now saying that such animal experiments are crude and unscientific. Animals often react to substances differently from humans, so animal tests give results that don't necessarily apply to people. In poisoning tests animals are often given much larger doses of a substance than humans would ever use.

What alternatives are there?

One alternative of course is not to produce any new ingredients – there are already thousands of ingredients for cosmetics – do we really need any more? Companies that produce 'cruelty-free' products use mild and natural ingredients or substances that are known to be safe because they have been used by people for many years.

As long as companies continue to produce new ingredients for cosmetics and other products there will be a need to test them for safety. The long-term answer, then, is to replace animal tests with humane ones. Humane experiments to replace all the standard safety tests for toxicity, or the skin and eye irritancy tests, already exist. And because they are based on human data they will provide much more reliable results. Write to us if you want a fact sheet on alternatives.

Guide to cruelty-free shopping

The best way to encourage cosmetics manufacturers to change their policy on animal testing is to use your consumer power and only buy 'cruelty-free' non-animal-tested products.

How many experiments?

No. of experiments (1993)

Cosmetics	3,838	77% increase from 1992
Household products	2,204	6% increase from 1992

Animals most used

Cosmetics testing:
mice, rats, guinea pigs, rabbits and fish.

Household product testing:
mice, rats, guinea pigs and rabbits.

The trouble is, buying 'cruelty-free' isn't as straight-forward as it first appears. The various 'cruelty-free' or 'animal-friendly' claims made by different companies can be pretty confusing. At present, there is no standard way of labelling products.

So, here is our brief guide:
Beware if labels say:
'Product not tested on animals.'

The ingredients might have been tested on animals.

'We (the company) do not perform tests on animals.'

The company's supplier or its parent company may have tested the product or ingredients on its behalf.

'Contains only natural ingredients.'

'Natural' or not, they may have been tested on animals.

'Environmentally friendly product.'

'Green' or 'environmentally friendly' products may have been tested on animals.

The main 'cruelty-free' policies are:

Fixed cut-off date

This means that the products do not contain any ingredients that have been tested on animals after a certain date. The 'cut-off date' varies between companies, but the best one to look for is 1978. The products may contain some ingredients that were tested on animals before the 'cut-off date'. But the important point is that the company is not supporting any animal testing that took place after that time. Animal Aid believes the 'cut-off date' policy is the better of the two policies.

Five year rule

This means that the product contains ingredients which have not been tested on animals during the previous five years. Ingredients which were tested on animals, say, six years before could be included. As it can take around five years for a newly tested ingredient to be used in a product anyway, this policy on its own will not be effective in putting a stop to animal tests. After all, an ingredient being tested today could be used by the manufacturer in five years' time.

Companies

Here are some manufacturers which have a fixed cut-off date policy. Their ranges are mostly available from health-food shops, but you may find some in supermarkets or department stores.

cosmetics:
Animal Aid (of course!)
Beauty Without Cruelty
Caurnie Soaps
Crimpers Pure Haircare
Daniel Field
Faith in Nature
Honesty Cosmetics
Montagne Jeunesse
Pure Plant Products
Weleda

household products:
ACDO
Caurnie Soaps
Clear Spring (Faith Products)
Ecover
HomeCare Technology
Honesty
Janco Sales Liquid Concentrate
Little Green Shop
Most of these companies have a mail-order service too.

If you would like addresses for any of these companies, write and tell us and we'll send you them. Please enclose an SAE.

Supermarket 'own brands' are often labelled as 'not tested on animals'. Ask for further details of their animal-testing policy and whether the products contain animal ingredients.

In brief

The golden rule is *check the label!*

Remember, most of the big companies that produce cosmetics and household products still use animal experiments and ingredients.

Unless a product has a label saying that it has not been tested on animals then you can assume it has.

On labels you should look for two things:

1. That neither the product nor its ingredients have been tested on animals.

2. That the product contains no animal ingredients.

Beware of animal ingredients

Watch out for animal ingredients in cosmetic products.

Soaps and creams are sometimes made with animal fats such as tallow and lard.

Shampoos can contain animal protein and some cosmetics contain gelatine, animal glycerine, collagen and placental cells which are all slaughterhouse products.

Expensive perfumes sometimes contain real musk (scraped from musk pods of the male musk deer), civet and castoreum (which are extracted from the anal sex glands of civet cats and beavers respectively).

This is only a summary. Contact us for a more comprehensive guide to cruelty-free cosmetics. See page 39 for address details.

You can also contact the Vegan Society (at 7 Battle Road, St Leonards on Sea, E Sussex TN37 7AA) for information on cruelty-free shopping (including household products and food stuffs)

© Animal Aid

Animal testing – your questions answered

The background

'What is meant by cosmetics?'

To most consumers the word cosmetics means lipsticks, mascaras, eyeshadows and face powder, but the legal definition is quite different and covers a much wider range of products. The majority of our industry's products are items such as toothpaste, soap, deodorants, skin and hair-care preparations; products used every day by practically everyone. All of these are applied directly to the external surface of the body, e.g. the skin or mouth. It is therefore essential that they are safe.

'What is safety testing?'

Safety testing involves a range of assessments which can include animal testing where no alternative can provide validated results. Within our industry, the safety of a finished product can generally be assessed from a knowledge of the ingredients and most finished products are not tested on animals. Where animal testing is necessary it is generally for new materials or combinations of ingredients which need to be more carefully evaluated.

'Are animals used for testing colour cosmetics?'

Animals are rarely used for safety testing colour cosmetics. The majority of companies active in the colour cosmetics market have a policy of not being involved with animal testing. This is because most new cosmetics tend to be based on the development of new colours, which can be achieved by using the existing palette of established colours together with existing ingredients.

'What is meant by "cruelty-free" and "not tested on animals"?'

The terms 'cruelty-free' and 'not tested on animals' are difficult to define as they are subject to a wide number of interpretations by different companies, organisations and regulatory bodies. Factors taken into account can include the origin of the ingredients and the time since the last known tests took place. Some companies base their 'cruelty-free' or 'not tested on animals' statements on the fact that neither they, nor their suppliers, have carried out or commission animal tests on finished products. Other companies base claims on a time frame of five or ten years, either on a fixed or rolling basis in relation to both the products and ingredients. There are also manufacturers who will not use ingredients which have been introduced since 1976 or 1978, these being the dates of introduction and implementation of the 1976 EC Directive. Customers should refer to individual company policy statements for details.

'Is the LD50 test used nowadays?'

The LD50 test is no longer used

by the cosmetics and toiletries industry.

This test was traditionally carried out to provide information on toxic effects of a substance when swallowed. The LD50 is calculated following the feeding of a large number of animals (usually rats) with a range of doses, some of which will cause death.

'Is any acute toxicity testing necessary?'

Most cosmetics are, by nature, unlikely to be harmful when swallowed, and manufacturers normally do not carry out any form of testing on finished product. Only in rare cases, where there is uncertainty, is it necessary to carry out any toxicity testing. This information is required to find out, for instance, whether a product could be harmful when swallowed by a child.

When some estimate of acute toxicity is necessary to provide assurance of consumer safety, companies generally use alternative procedures such as a 'limit' test. Here the dose administered is related to the amount likely to be ingested by man and is usually between two and five grams per kg. Generally, ten animals or fewer are used. If, as is normally the case with cosmetics, there are no serious adverse effects, no further testing is required. Where death is not required as an end point animals can be humanely killed at the first sign of distress and therefore suffering is considerably reduced.

In 1984 the CTPA Council issued a statement urging its member companies to press their suppliers of ingredients to carry out 'limit' tests rather than LD50 tests, to establish safety. The industry welcomes the recent EC moves to adopt the so-called 'fixed dose procedure' as an officially accepted method. Here death is not required as an end point and animal distress is considerably reduced.

'What about the Draize eye test?'

There is a great deal of false information in circulation concerning eye irritancy testing. The classic Draize eye test, where an ingredient is placed into one of the eyes of several animals (usually rabbits) and the effects observed over a period of 1 to 72 hours, is not used for cosmetic and toiletry testing.

'Is any eye testing necessary?'

The eye is a very important and vulnerable organ and, because many products are applied to the eye area, manufacturers must exercise great care to ensure that no damage can arise.

Extreme irritancy and corrosiveness can be assessed by in-vitro (non-animal) methods. Where confirmation of low or nil irritancy response is required, test procedures involving the dilution of substances can be used so that mild response is produced. A single animal is used in the initial test.

Alternative laboratory procedures not using animals are being implemented by a number of CTPA member companies and are already used as preliminary screening procedures, but no other techniques have so far proved satisfactory in all circumstances. Research is continuing.

New products

Animal suffering versus human safety

The RSPCA has long opposed the animal testing of cosmetics, but is equally concerned about the many other types of products which involve tests on animals. The Society wants to increase public awareness of this issue. Such awareness is vital if animal suffering is to be reduced. This article provides information on the use of animals for testing a wide range of everyday products and environmental pollutants. The RSPCA accepts the need to safeguard human health and to protect the environment, but is appalled that so many laboratory animals suffer as a consequence.

Background factors

The use of animals for 'testing' has been a major issue with the public and the media in recent years. Most of the concern has focused on the testing of cosmetics. It is not generally realised that animals are also used for testing the safety of other products (or their ingredients) that are used daily in the home and garden, in agriculture, at work and in industry.

In general it is only new substances which have to be tested. Therefore pressure to produce new 'improved' products, together with demands for their safety, increases the pressure for tests on animals. This condemns animals to death in tests designed to safeguard the health and safety of consumers and workers in industry, and to protect the environment. There is great concern about animals suffering in safety testing, so consumers need to be aware of the consequences for animals resulting from pressure for new products.

This article answers some of the many questions asked about safety tests on animals, including: the types of substances tested, the laws that are involved and what can be done to help animals.

There are many misconceptions about the extent of animal testing; which substances are tested, why they are tested; which laws are involved and what can be done. Here we answer some of these questions.

Which substances are tested?

The types of products that involve tests on animals are given in the Home Office Statistics of Scientific Procedures on Living Animals published each year. These are shown below together with the approximate number of animals used in 1991. The 1987 figures (in brackets) are given as a comparison. This was the first year statistics were collected under the Animals (Scientific Procedures) Act 1986.

Household products – 2,800 (6,900)
Chemicals used in agriculture and gardens e.g. pesticides, herbicides and fungicides – 77,600 (77,500)
Substances used in industry – 87,200 (70,300)
Food additives – 10,800 (3,200)
Cosmetics – 3,000 (14,500)
Also included under the broad category of 'safety testing' are:
Environmental pollutants – 58,200 (28,200)
Tobacco and alcohol –500 (1,200)

Why are substances tested?

Substances are tested to see how safe they are; what precautions are needed when using them; what to do in the event of accidents, and to assess any adverse effects on the environment. Of course animals are not the same as humans. The results of tests are used as a guide to human risk. In some cases where substances are actually intended to be toxic (poisonous), e.g. pesticides and weed-killers, tests are done to assess the levels of risk involved.

Are animal tests specified by law?

Safety testing is required under a variety of UK and international legislation relating to human health and safety and to the protection of the environment. Depending on the legislation and class of substance, animal tests are either specified or implied – for example they may be done because it is known that the authorities rely on them in order to make decisions about whether or not a substance can be marketed.

Which laws are involved?

Safety testing is carried out under UK laws such as:

Agriculture (Poisonous Substances) Act 1952

Health and Safety at Work Act 1974

Food and Drugs Act 1955 (Amendments 1981 and 1982)

Some cosmetic and toiletry ingredients may be tested under the Medicines Act 1968.

Substances are also subject to European laws such as:

The Classification, Packaging and Labelling of Dangerous Substances Regulations 1984

Since manufacturers export products from the UK and Europe to countries such as Japan and the USA they must comply with the testing regulations of these countries. In many cases these are more rigorous than European requirements.

The animal tests themselves are also regulated and controlled by law – the Animals (Scientific Procedures) Act 1986.

Which animals are used?

The majority of animals used in safety testing are rodents. In 1991, 179,075 rodents were used together with 53,638 fish, 8,358 birds, 7,371 rabbits, 877 dogs, 251 primates, 177 sheep, small numbers (under 50) of other farm animals and 5 cats. Rabbits, rats and guinea pigs are used for testing cosmetics.

Do tests cause suffering?

In the UK, tests have been modified in recent years to reduce the suffering involved. However, pain, suffering or distress will undoubtedly result in many cases.

Can human volunteers be used?

In the case of cosmetics and toiletries finished products are tested on human volunteers. However, humans could not be used in most of the tests carried out on animals. These tests do not just consist of trying out a new skin cream. The idea is to see if damage is caused by a particular substance. For example, tests must show whether a substance is poisonous in long-term use, whether it causes cancer or damages unborn babies. Society considers it unethical to submit humans to such tests, even if people were prepared to risk life and limb.

Can alternatives to animals be used in tests?

Unfortunately there are not yet alternatives to all the different types of tests required. A lot of research to develop alternatives is being done, particularly on tests such as the Draize eye irritancy test. This test should be replaceable, but there are many frustrating problems. Once an alternative is developed it has to be validated (shown to work reliably in different laboratories). It then has to be approved by the people that make testing regulations. This can take many years, even though the alternative tests may be just as good as, or even better than, the animal tests.

'Cruelty-free' labels

Very few products, other than cosmetics, are labelled as 'not tested on animals' or 'cruelty-free'. 'Cruelty-free' products are very popular but different companies have different criteria for such labels and many of

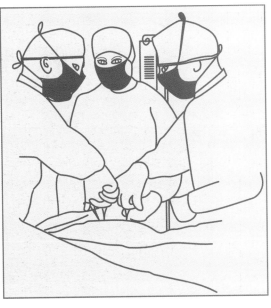

the claims made are misleading. For example, it is usually only ingredients which must be tested and not the finished product. Labels stating that the product has not been tested on animals therefore mean very little.

The RSPCA has set its own criteria for defining 'cruelty-free'. This, and other issues surrounding product labelling, are set out in the Society's booklet *Guide to products not tested on animals*.

What do consumers think?

Latest opinion polls conducted by the RSPCA show a clear rejection of animal testing on household products and cosmetics, with 95% opposed to animal testing of household products, and 96% opposed to animal testing for cosmetics and toiletries.

The way forward

The way forward must be to ensure safety without suffering by:

– developing, validating and adopting alternative tests which do not use living animals

– questioning the extent of testing currently required

– questioning the need for so many new products.

The RSPCA is dismayed by the lack of progress on this issue. Both industry and government need to take a more co-ordinated approach to the problem. Those government regulatory bodies who define the tests required should take a more flexible attitude to risk-assessment and safety testing regulations.

Obviously, while human health must not be compromised, these bodies must be more prepared to accept validated alternatives together with the safety records of established substances. Finally, the Government should be prepared to invest more funds in 'alternatives' research. For 1991/ 1992 the amount of money made available for the Home Office's Animal Procedures Committee to fund research into refinement and replacement methods was only £215,000.

The Society urges all concerned in government and industry to give this matter the most urgent attention.

© RSPCA

What's wrong with animal rights?

We call ourselves 'animal lovers'. We donate millions of pounds each year to animal charities, often without knowing what they do. We are appalled by those nations whose inhabitants happily eat dogs or cats. Many people (especially children), if asked, would say they think animals should have 'rights'.

But what are 'animal rights'? What is the difference between animal 'rights' and animal welfare? And does it matter?

Animal welfare is based on humane care. The premise is that animals can be used to benefit humans, but their use carries responsibilities and obligations to the animals. These include appropriate housing, feeding, watering, health care and the alleviation of pain and suffering.

Animal 'rights' philosophy, however, is not concerned with humane care and use of animals. It focuses on whether humans have any right at all to use animals as resources, and what 'rights' animals are entitled to as living, feeling beings. Animal 'rights' philosophy is based on the belief that animals may not be used for any purpose by humans – that animals are not 'ours' to eat, wear, work, or use in any way.

Animal 'rights' is big business

Animal 'rights' is big business. Millions of pounds every year are spent on salaries, administration and 'campaigning'. A well-meaning donor may expect his contribution to be used to feed or treat neglected animals – in most cases he'd be wrong. This fact has attracted comment in the United States. According to federal tax returns for 1995, no less than 13 executives of the Humane

Society of the United States (HSUS) earned more than $70,000 in 1994. HSUS chief executive, John Hoyt, earned a whopping $226,704 while Paul Irwin, HSUS president, earned $210,267. Of the 53 animal organisations listed in the National Charities Information Bureau guidelines, 11 spend more than 40% on overheads and fund-raising costs, and 8 had amassed assets of over $10 million.

The International Fund for Animal Welfare (IFAW) expects to make £10 million in the UK alone this year and recently advertised for a new chief executive, offering a salary of up to £60,000 plus benefits. IFAW is not recognised as a charity in any country in which it operates. Its founder, Brian Davies, draws an annual salary of over £60,000 from IFAW (UK) for his part-time duties. He is believed to earn similar sums from IFAW (US) and the other IFAW companies in Canada, Australia and Europe. In 1995, IFAW spent nearly £2 million on an advertising campaign in support of an anti-hunting Bill. IFAW could certainly claim to have raised the profile of animal issues, but it is harder in the UK to identify any substantial practical benefits delivered to animals.

Those who support animal 'rights' do NOT love animals more – they love people less. Don't just take our word for it – this is what they say...

The life of an ant and the life of my child should be granted equal consideration.
(Michael Fox, HSUS)

I could understand anyone who was so angered and troubled by animal abuse that they were driven to take a life.
(Robin Webb, ALF Animal Liberation Front)

We are not especially 'interested in' animals. Neither of us had ever been inordinately fond of dogs, cats or horses in the way that many people are. We didn't 'love' animals.
(Peter Singer, who coined the term 'animal liberation')

Not only are the philosophies of animal rights and animal welfare separated by irreconcilable differences... the enactment of animal welfare measures actually impedes the achievement of animal rights... Welfare reforms, by their very nature, can only serve to retard the pace at which animal rights' goals are achieved.
(Gary Francione and Tom Regan, *The Animals' Agenda*)

Pet ownership is an absolutely abysmal situation brought about by human manipulation.
(Ingrid Newkirk, PETA)

Let us allow the dog to disappear from our brick and concrete jungles – from our firesides, from the leather nooses and chains by which we enslave it.
(John Bryant League Against Cruel Sports)

How does this affect me?

The animal 'rights' movement is making a determined effort to force the philosophy of animal 'rights' on a society that doesn't understand it. Instead of preaching their views openly and honestly, many of its supporters try to force their views on the public through emotive and misleading propaganda, emotional blackmail, and even terrorism. They ask people to show their love of animals by cultivating hatred for those seen as animal 'abusers' – farmers, scientists, hunters.

Tragically, this philosophy can only increase the inevitable suffering of wild animals, while farmed and domestic animals could cease to exist. Leaving animals in the hands of nature means they die from predation, fighting, accident or disease. All of these cause considerable suffering and cannot be avoided. If we fail to manage nature by controlling numbers and preserving habitat, more species will be lost forever.

The struggle for animal 'rights' is not just dishonest and counter-productive. It is costing British industry and the taxpayer hundreds of millions of pounds a year. It diverts essential funding from medical and veterinary research, the fight against crime, and animal welfare.

Don't be fooled or misled. Ask questions, check the facts. Support animal welfare and support sensible and responsible conservation of our environment. But animal 'rights' are wrong!

In opposition to animal rights

The animal rights movement illustrates the incoherent nature of a moral passion become immoral by virtue of its extremism. In the name of the laudable quality of humaneness, the use of animals for food, clothing and medical experimentation is prohibited. Research that could save your child's life, or save you from an excruciating disease, is declared unethical. The result is inhumanity towards man.
(Charles Griswold, Professor of Philosophy, Howard University, USA)

To suppose that they (animal rights) are inherent in some value or quality in animal life as such poses the further sharp question, which animals? All, or only some? And if all, on what grounds do we designate some as vermin?
(Dr John Hapgood, former Archbishop of York)

While there are sports for horses the existing, in general extremely high, level of their care can be assured. Should the animal rights lobby eventually manage to prevent horse sports then the lives of a vast number of horses – and people – will, without doubt, be catastrophically poorer.
(Lucinda Green champion 3-day event rider)

We have no duty of care towards any specific wild animal – to assume otherwise is to deny that it is wild. Duties towards animals are assumed but are not imposed. Hence there is a real moral difference between the person who allows his terrier to kill wild rats and the person who keeps tame rats for his terrier to kill.
(Roger Scruton, philosopher, *Animal Rights and Wrongs*)

Photo: League Against Cruel Sports

Hunting

Information from Animal Aid

Every year in our countryside fox-hunters kill about 13,000 foxes for sport. Whereas you or I might watch a football match or go for a swim, these people enjoy themselves by chasing and killing foxes.

The red fox is a small wild dog that lives mainly on earthworms, rodents, beetles and carrion. Being a close relative of the domestic dog, it can feel fear and pain in just the same way.

Foxes are highly adaptable animals and many of them have moved into our towns and cities. They have no natural predators and largely regulate or control their own population. The number of fox cubs born each year depends on the number of vixens that breed and this depends on the amount of food available and the size and number of territories.

Do you think this is fair?

30 riders (including the huntmaster, huntsman with a gun, two whippers-in and hunt followers on horseback), 30 horses, 40 hounds, several terrier, men in Land-Rovers with terrier dogs and spades and several hunt followers in cars . . .

versus

. . . one small fox

Actually, only a very small minority of people go hunting. And the vast majority of people (80% in recent opinion polls) are against fox-hunting and want to see it banned.

What's going on?

The hunting of wild animals (red deer, wild boar, hares and wolves) with dogs was the traditional sport of kings and rich landowners for centuries. When wild boars and wolves became extinct and the forests and deer herds declined, hunters sought a new quarry – the fox. Fox-hunting as we know it today has only existed for the last 250 years. The official fox-hunting season begins on 1st November and runs through until April, although some hunts even go on into May. Fox cubs are usually born in March, which means that pregnant and nursing vixens are often hunted and killed. From August to September, fox-hunters go cub-hunting. The vixen and her young cubs are trapped in the wood where they were born in the spring and hunted down. During 'cubbing', new young foxhounds are trained to hunt and kill. The dogs don't hunt foxes by natural instinct, but must be trained and encouraged to do so. Pets and farm animals have been killed by hunts rampaging over private land and many foxhounds die chasing their quarry over roads and railway lines. Hunts also slaughter over 10,000 hounds every year. Most are considered too old to hunt after six years and are shot (there are no retirement homes for old hounds!) whilst younger hounds will be killed if they don't fit in with the rest of the pack or aren't good enough at hunting.

So why do people go hunting?

'We do it for the ride…it's the best way to get a good gallop.'

But horse riders can go for a gallop any time. They don't have to chase foxes to do it!

'We've been hunting for hundreds of years. . .it's a fine old rural tradition.'

Times have changed and we have stopped lots of barbaric things that people used to do in the past like dog-fighting, bear-baiting, slavery and sending children up chimneys to clean them! However, some barbaric 'traditions' like fox-hunting still continue.

'Fox-hunters preserve the countryside – they are conservationists.'

Terrorising and killing wildlife is a funny form of conservation! Hunting does not protect the countryside. Woodlands, hedgerows, wild meadows and ponds are all disappearing at an alarming rate and real conservation groups such as Friends of the Earth are campaigning for laws to preserve wildlife habitats and protect wild animals.

'Foxes are pests – they need to be controlled.'

Foxes are often accused of killing poultry, but as most poultry today are kept indoors in intensive 'battery' conditions, few are in any danger from foxes. Chickens that are free-range can be securely locked up at night to keep them safe. Foxes are also sometimes accused of killing lambs, although this is rare. They are scavengers by nature, so tend to take lambs that have already died of natural causes. Many new-born lambs do die, especially if they are kept on the hills in cold, wet weather.

Foxes are not pests; they help maintain the balance of nature and are beneficial to many farmers because they help control rabbits, rats and mice. They are part of our countryside and of our natural ecology.

'Hunting is the most humane way to control foxes.'

All the different ways that are used to kill foxes such as snaring, shooting, gassing, trapping and poisoning are cruel and unnecessary. The whole point of hunting is that the 'chase' lasts as long as possible. That is why the hounds are bred for stamina, not speed. Not only is the chase exhausting and terrifying but the final kill is violent and painful. If the fox tries to take refuge underground, for example in its earth or in a drain, then small fierce terrier dogs will be sent down to fight with it and drive it out to its death.

Actually. . .people who hunt do it because they enjoy it

. . .and enjoyment is not really a good enough reason for terrorising and killing wild animals. Foxes aren't the only animals that are hunted. Other forms of hunting still legal in this country include: deer-hunting, hare-hunting, hare-coursing and mink-hunting. Some people still take part in the illegal 'sports' of badger-baiting, dog-fighting and cock-fighting, and animal rights groups together with the police are working to stamp out these activities.

But you can help stop them!

Join our campaign to make hunting a crime instead of a sport. Here are some things you can do right now:
1. For further information either write to us at Animal Aid or contact the League Against Cruel Sports.

(Don't forget to include a self-addressed envelope.)
Animal Aid, The Old Chapel, Bradford Street, Tonbridge, Kent TN9 1AW. Tel: 01732 364546
League Against Cruel Sports, Sparling House, 83/84 Union Street, London SE1 1SG

2. Write to your MP and ask him/her to help ban hunting. You can find out who your MP is from your local library.

3. Many councils have already banned hunting on public land. Write to your local council and ask them to ban hunting if they haven't already done so. Get the address from your library.

Shooting sports – live quarry

We all find different things enjoyable and for many reasons. Simply because a particular sport doesn't appeal to us, rarely do we seek to prevent others from practising it – even if we do not understand the enjoyment that activity gives. In this country around one million people enjoy the sport of shooting, be it game shooting, deer stalking, rough shooting or wildfowling (shooting of ducks and geese). This sport provides employment for around 50,000 people and £600m in government revenue.

Yet this is an activity against which people actively campaign. Is it fair to want to stop a significant number of individuals – more than say, who play rugby – practising a sport they enjoy without fully understanding the issues surrounding shooting?

How can shooting birds and animals be called a sport?

Shooting live quarry has for centuries traditionally been called a sport. A sport does not have to be a competition or a team game – think

The British Association
for Shooting & Conservation

of climbing or sailing. Some types of shooting, for example, deer stalking, involve specialist skills of field craft. Clay shooting develops a sense of timing and hand-to-eye co-ordination. Like most sports, shooting develops particular abilities and mental and physical fitness.

How can anyone enjoy killing an animal or a bird?

Enjoyment is a complex human emotion which is why we are sometimes at a loss to explain exactly why we enjoy something. We may give numerous reasons. For example, there are many reasons why people enjoy playing football. There may be a primary reason – one person may say it is because of the teamwork involved, another may say he likes running around using up excess energy, another may say he likes the skill of controlling the ball, another may say he likes competing against another side – but usually it is a

combination of these things that make up an indefinable whole. Likewise the reasons why people enjoy shooting live quarry are many and diverse – a love of being in the countryside, a pleasure in bringing food to the table, satisfaction in good marksmanship and a clean kill of the quarry, liking the companionship and social side of the sport and so on. It is a fact that people enjoy it. The enjoyment does not come from a desire to satisfy a blood-lust or to inflict cruelty on a living creature. The sport of shooting is strictly governed by a code of ethics and practice and the ambition of all shooters is a clean kill that causes no pain or distress to the quarry. Why not talk to people who shoot about why they find it enjoyable?

Why can't people get as much pleasure from shooting clay targets? Why do they have to shoot live creatures?

Many people in this country are great enthusiasts of clay shooting and it is an important sport in its own right. Again it is a matter of preference.

All the reasons stated above for enjoying football could be applied to, say, rugby but still people prefer football to rugby (and vice versa) – they are different sports. Shooting birds and animals gets you involved in the management of the countryside – many shooters are also conservation workers. The benefits to the environment of shooting live quarry are recognised by the statutory conservation bodies in this country. Clay shooting does not have this dimension and you can't eat a clay pigeon.

Do people eat what they shoot?

Yes. Shooters in effect harvest meat for their table – whether it be rabbit, pheasant, pigeon, duck, goose or venison. This meat is wholly organic and comes from animals and birds that have lived healthy lives roaming wild, some after a controlled rearing period but not all. Consider the meat, eggs and dairy produce we eat that comes from the supermarket. We know that much of this comes from intensively farmed animals. Compare the life of the pheasant in the woodland and the deer on the hill to that of the battery chicken or the intensively reared pig.

Deer are lovely creatures – how can people want to shoot these animals?

Any creature needs a habitat in which to live. In this country much of our landscape is now covered with housing, roads and industrial development and as a result there is not enough habitat to support the deer population. If deer are left unmanaged then visible consequences will soon occur. It is a fact that for instance in the Scottish highlands many deer die of starvation each year. Deer are therefore managed through culling to maintain a balanced, healthy population which has sufficient food to survive. Organisations such as the RSPB on one of their reserves in Scotland shoot deer to prevent them from starving to death

Isn't it cruel to shoot animals and birds?

No. Shooters operate under a strict code of ethics and practice and all strive for a clean kill. No shooter wants to inflict pain on its quarry. An injured bird or animal will be dispatched as quickly and humanely as possible. It is widely accepted that birds and animals simply do not have developed emotional responses in the way humans do. A pheasant has no conception of a shotgun and a deer is as likely to run from a photographer and his camera as from a stalker and his rifle. Greater distress and disturbance to wildlife is often caused by walkers and dogs. The dictionary defines cruelty as 'the indifference to, or the taking pleasure in, another's suffering'. This does not apply to sporting shooting. No responsible shooting person is ever indifferent to the possibility of his or her quarry suffering or takes any pleasure in it.

What right does anyone have to kill an animal or bird?

Shooters have a legal right to shoot live quarry within the restrictions laid down by the law. Shooting is a well-organised, sustainable and wise use of a natural resource

Unfortunately it is less and less understood. It is widely acknowledged to be directly beneficial to wildlife and its habitat and is greatly enjoyed by a significant number of people.

No shooter believes he has the right to shoot quarry gratuitously or indiscriminately, but rather takes a harvest from the land in the same way a farmer takes his harvest and ensures that his crop is sustainable.

The difficulty with moral questions and dilemmas is that we have no facts but only beliefs – which may be very strongly held. Before condemning sport that does so much for the countryside we all enjoy and is a natural way of life for a good proportion of people in this country we must be careful to take into account all the factors. Are we guilty of hypocrisy – do we condemn the shooter because he enjoys his sport rather than the farmer who provides himself with an income from killing and rearing animals? Is there a difference? Do you eat meat, dairy products or eggs? Where do they come from? Do you drive a car? The AA tells us one-fifth of all pheasants are killed by cars. Do you keep a cat? Cats in the UK kill around 210 million animals and birds a year.

Sporting shooting puts a great deal back into the countryside, from habitat management, bird-refuge monitoring, creation of wildflower meadows to protecting rare water beetles. Talk to people who shoot and find out for yourself how shooting looks after the countryside.

© *The British Association for Shooting & Conservation*

Photo: British Association for Shooting & Conservation

Bloodsports in Britain

Information from the St Andrew Animal Fund

Introduction

In the distant past before neolithic man became a farmer, hunting was an important method of obtaining food. It was probably also a defence against animals that were dangerous or competed with him for food and shelter. It was a necessary activity, not a mere amusement. This is not to deny that from very early times successful hunters took pride and pleasure in their exploits. These sentiments may well have inspired the palaeolithic artists whose wonderful paintings of animals can still be seen in French and Spanish caves, though religion and magic were probably more compelling influences.

It is clear that in sophisticated modern Britain hunting, once a useful activity, has become something very different: a pastime which sometimes masquerades as a service to agriculture, but is in fact a considerable nuisance to it. It does not effect any useful control of wild animals that cannot be more efficiently and more humanely achieved by other methods, if of course control is ever necessary.

Some measure of cruelty was unavoidable in the killing of animals in the hard lives and primitive society of palaeolithic hunters. One would perhaps have looked in vain for any feelings of kindness or pity towards their quarry. But at least they were actuated by the need to feed and protect their families and themselves. No such need actuates the men, women and children who hunt for sport in Britain today and that is why their cruelty is more culpable than that of our primitive ancestors and their callousness greater, their purpose being their own pleasure. They prefer a long hunt to a short one; in other words, the more prolonged the hunted animal's torment before it is caught and killed the better they are pleased.

Leslie Pine, former managing editor of *The Shooting Times*, who incidentally resigned because he could not endure the constant theme of killing wild creatures, said of bloodsports that they were no longer necessary in Britain and that: 'Blood shedding for the sheer fun of it is unworthy of any intelligent man or woman, and is indeed, whatever its name, exactly on a par with the torturing of a cat or dog by a gang of louts in a back street.'[1]

We now look at some of the bloodsports of Britain.

Fox-hunting

The fox

The population of foxes in Britain in early January each year numbers 200,000. During this month foxes mate and by March/April they will have produced an average 300,000 cubs. The cubs leave their parents in October/November. The staple diet of the fox is beetles, frogs, rabbits, wild birds, carrion, rats and mice.

The population of foxes in a given area is governed naturally by territorial jealousies and food availability. Research work carried out by Dr David Macdonald of Oxford University found on average across the countryside four adults (one dog and three vixens) per 1,000 acres.

The hunt

There are approximately 200 fox-hunts currently operating in Britain. They hunt either two or four days each week and are accompanied on their excursions by hunt followers who follow the hunt either on foot or by car. 'Terrier men' also accompany the hunt in case a fox 'goes to ground'. On average each fox-hunt keeps sixty dogs. These hounds are bred for stamina not speed.

The main hunting season is from November until April which means that many heavily pregnant and nursing fox mothers are hunted. However, in August, prior to the main hunting season, the hunters commence 'cub-hunting'.

Cub-hunting

The purpose of cub-hunting is to take young inexperienced hounds out with older hounds prior to the start of the season in order to 'blood' them and allow them to get the taste for chasing and killing foxes. Their quarry is the fox cubs born in the spring and now six months old.

The hunt, aware of the location of a fox – say in a wood – surrounds it with horses and riders. The huntsman takes the hounds into the wood to chase and kill the cubs. If a cub breaks from the wood, the riders chase it back. Any adult fox attempting to escape is allowed to do so since it will provide 'sport' for the hunt at a later date. A former Master of Foxhounds provides an insight into the end of a typical cub-hunt. The cubs, he said: 'continued to blunder about in a kind of terrified daze at the strange petrifying invasion of their quiet sanctuary, and it was not long before they were literally driven into the very mouths of the hounds, and torn up piecemeal, despite the valiant efforts of the vixen to distract the attention of the pack by leaving the covert upwind in the hope that her stronger scent would draw hounds away'.[2]

It is also well known that many fox cubs are dug out from their earths and either given to the hounds or savaged where they lie.

The chase

After weeks of training the hounds

are ready for the main hunting season and at the beginning of November fox-hunting begins in earnest.

Most hunts gather in the late morning. During the early hours of the morning an 'earth stopper' will have been out to block up the entrances of known fox earths in the area that is to be hunted. The fox, being a nocturnal animal, returns after spending the night searching for food only to discover that it is unable to find refuge underground and therefore has to lie up 'above ground'.

The hunt moves off to the location and the hounds are sent in to flush out the fox. Soon the chase is on and in the early stages the fox easily outpaces the hounds. The terrified animal attempts to lose the pack by running through woods, across railway lines, through flocks of sheep and, in desperation, through gardens. It is not uncommon for hounds in full cry to attack and kill cats and other domestic animals.

The fox not being a natural prey species is not physically evolved for a prolonged pursuit and after about an hour it is either caught and savaged by the pack of hounds ('broken-up' as the hunt call it) or goes to ground in an unblocked earth or badger sett. But even underground the fox is not safe – the terrier men who follow the hunt in vehicles are called in.

Terrier men

The terrier men are specifically used by the hunt for foxes that have gone to ground. These men put their terrier dogs down the earth in an attempt to 'bolt' the fox and force it to run for its life again. If the fox refuses to move, perhaps because it is physically incapable (or is defending its cubs), then the terriers keep it under attack thereby allowing the terrier men to dig down to it. When the fox is exposed it is either shot, forced to run or thrown alive to the waiting hounds. As a former Master of Foxhounds states:

'Fox-hunting above all, is organised torture leading to murder.'[3]

Terrier men when not employed by hunts during the hunting season persecute foxes throughout the year. It is interesting to note that from courtroom appearances of those found guilty of dog-fighting, a large percentage are from a background of fox-hunting, terrier-working and badger-baiting.

Some related points answered

Is death instantaneous?

It is often claimed by the hunt that foxes which are caught by hounds are always killed instantaneously. This statement is untrue as the author of this publication will bear witness. Without taking into account the physical exhaustion, pain and sheer terror the animals suffer during the chase, of the fourteen foxes he has seen killed by a hunt, only two seemed to die immediately. The other twelve called and screamed as one hound grabbed its share of the fox and the others theirs until some time later in between this tugging and pulling the animal finally died. The author has also seen the head, feet and tail (brush) cut off as trophies before the animal was finally thrown to the hounds. He has also witnessed on many occasions a hunt which has failed to kill that day take its hounds

to a known fox earth and, with the aid of terrier men, dig out and kill the fox. This was done solely to get a 'kill'. Bagged foxes, some with their pads slit with a penknife to slow them down, are also known to be released in front of the hounds – so much for the 'sporting chance'.

Control?

If there is any justification for fox-hunts it would be that they act as a form of control on fox numbers. The following is a summary of fox-killing figures:

Snared	50 – 100,000
Shot	50 – 100,000
Road accidents	50 – 100,000
Terrier men	25 – 50,000
Fox-hunting	12 – 13,000[4]

It is clear that fox-hunting makes little contribution to the control of fox numbers. It could be argued that if foxes were not persecuted by humans, their numbers would remain constant since their survival is dependent on food and territory available. In other words, nature would rule. If a rogue fox should ever have to be controlled then live cage trapping or shooting by a skilled marksman with the appropriate weapon are the methods to employ.

Other facts which clearly demonstrate that fox-hunts are established for the pleasure of killing and not for the purpose of controlling fox numbers (or in support of conservation) are:

- The hunt provides artificial earths in which the foxes can breed and raise their cubs.
- The hunt makes sure there are enough foxes left to breed at the end of each hunting season.
- Fox cubs are brought from other areas to bolster the population in a heavily hunted area.

References
1. *After Their Blood,* Leslie Pine, p.13.
2. *Against Hunting,* p.43.
3. *A Master of Hounds Speaks,* Robert Churchwood, p.3.
4. *Wildlife Protection,* publ. League Against Cruel Sports, p.14.

This is fox-hunting

Country sports are good for the countryside!

Fox-hunting is the pursuit of the wild fox with a pack of hounds. Man has been controlling foxes since he started to farm animals, but the hunting of foxes with hounds for sport became popular over 200 years ago.

The fox is a pest and its population needs to be controlled. Individuals and organisations concerned with farming and the management of the countryside recognise this fact. Responsible fox management includes maintaining a healthy population at a level at which it can thrive without threatening livestock or other wildlife. Fox-hunting is the most natural method of management: by its nature, it takes out the old, sick and injured foxes, and there is no risk of wounding. If the fox is caught, it is killed within seconds. If the fox goes to ground, either it will be left unharmed or the landowner may ask that it be killed by the hunt's terrier-man. The strict rules governing terrier work laid down by the Masters of Foxhounds Association (MFHA) ensure there is no unnecessary suffering. Fox-hunting does not just help control fox numbers. Land-owners with an interest in fox-hunting plant and maintain coverts, woodlands and copses for the benefit of all wildlife. Few farmers want to see the fox exterminated, but those who support hunting are more inclined to tolerate foxes on their land, as long as their numbers are controlled.

The fox

In rural areas of the UK, the red fox is in very good shape.

After 200 years of organised hunting, it is a perfectly conserved species. The British fox commands respect, but should not command sentimentality. Being an opportunist

predator, the fox will kill poultry, wildfowl, new-born lambs and piglets beyond the needs of its staple diet of small wild mammals, insects and worms.

The fox is a hunter and covers considerable distances hunting for food or in search of a mate. Like all wild animals when threatened, the fox attempts to put an adequate 'flight distance' between itself and a potential enemy. This is a natural survival instinct.

Hunting the fox

Each hunt has its own designated area called the hunt country. The hunt meets at a predetermined place and moves off to a 'draw', a particular woodland or other habitat where foxes are likely to be found. The only people involved with the hunting of the fox are the huntsman and his assistants, called Whippers-In. Mounted followers (the Field), under the control of the Field Master, are kept far enough away from the pack to ensure hounds can work unhindered. Between 30 and 40 hounds (15 and 20 'couple') hunt on a given day. Hounds are bred for intelligence, speed, stamina, voice and 'nose' (sense of smell). They follow the scent of a fox which may be quite some distance away. When the fox is killed, the pack will often eat the corpse. This has led to the

false belief that the hounds tear a live fox to pieces. This is a myth.

Seasons

Hunting is the only form of fox control that recognises a closed season.

Cub-hunting, or autumn hunting: August/September – October.

The word 'cub' is misleading. The foxes may be less than a year old but are, by this time, fully grown, and living and hunting independently. The objectives of cub-hunting are to cull some foxes and to disperse others, ensuring there are not too many in one area. Hounds hunt by instinct but during this period they learn to hunt only foxes. *Fox-hunting: November – March/April*

The duration of the season varies according to the nature of the farming in the area.

Call-outs: usually spring

A farmer who is losing lambs, piglets or poultry may ask the hunt to track and kill the guilty fox. This is a service for farmers, not sport.

'There is no doubt . . . that foxes can be damaging and indiscriminate predators of birds and other animals . . . Control methods must remain available to those suffering economic damage from foxes.'

(Labour Party policy document *Wildlife in the Countryside*, 1991)

Questions and answers

Surely, a ban on hunting would benefit the fox?

No. There is no doubt that more foxes would be killed by unregulated or perhaps illegal means. To quote a former Chief Executive of the League Against Cruel Sports: 'I do not wish hunting to be replaced by other forms of fox killing which may be crueller and take more fox numbers. Where is the overall gain for the fox?'

Is the case for fox control overstated?
No. Fox predation can cause significant lamb losses. Scientific estimates vary from 0.5% to 5.2%. Even at 2%, the cost to a typical hill farmer with 1,500 ewes is over £1,000 per year. Without control, predation may increase considerably.

What would be the consequences of a ban on fox-hunting?
Over 33,000 people whose jobs directly or indirectly depend on fox-hunting would be out of work. Some 12,000 foxhounds would have no future as they are working pack dogs and would not make suitable pets. There would be less incentive for farmers to conserve wildlife habitat.

Is drag hunting an alternative to foxhunting?
No. The Masters of Draghounds Association has made it clear that drag hunting is purely an equestrian sport, with no utilitarian value nor attraction for the foot followers. Drag hunting plays no part in wildlife management or conservation.

Is fox-hunting becoming more popular?
Yes. Fox-hunting has never been more popular. There are 196 registered packs of foxhounds in the UK supported by more than 41,000 riders and over 160,000 foot or car followers. Independent research shows that 95% of those opposed to fox-hunting admit to no knowledge of nor interest in the subject.
© British Field Sports Society

The ethics of shooting

Animal rights

This is a very big issue and not one to be dealt with lightly. But there are a few points worth considering to begin with.

It is important to remember that virtually every square metre of the British countryside, from the tops of the mountains to the foreshore of the coast, has been influenced by humans to a greater or lesser extent.

Those few species of birds and animals that are hunted and shot rely to a great extent on man-made habitats for their abundant existence in the first place. In many cases it can be shown that where certain birds and their habitats (grey partridges and red grouse for example) are managed and shot for sport, that is where they will be found at their most numerous and successful.

The hunter is simply making use of a sustainable resource and taking a harvest but ensuring that the overall population remains stable or increases.

Some people feel that, in spite of this, humans do not have the 'right' actually to take the life of an individual bird or animal. If followed to its conclusion this argument would mean that animals should no longer be farmed for meat or their products.

The taking of a bird or animal's

B|A|S|C The British Association
for Shooting & Conservation

life is obviously a matter of individual conscience and applies to everyone who eats meat and not just to the sportsman.

Human rights

Such extreme opinions do raise the question of the rights of people to undertake activities for sport and pleasure.

Shooting is a sustainable use of a natural resource which has environmental and economic benefits. It is widely acknowledged, not least by the Labour, Liberal Democrat and Conservative parties, to be directly beneficial to wildlife and its habitats. It is also greatly enjoyed by 600,000 people in Britain.

Is it then right to suggest that all shooting should be stopped because another group of people have different views and have no wish to take part themselves?

When people are taking part in a legitimate activity, such as shooting, can it be right that others who do not agree with the sport should try physically to stop them shooting – possibly by using violence themselves?

Conclusion

Often, without thinking, the sport of country shooting can be viewed as simply 'another **bloodsport**'. To lump it together with past practices such as bear-baiting and cock-fighting is inappropriate. The sport has a complex historical background, and is steeped in tradition, but it has moved with the times. It now provides a working example of sustainable management, a term coined only recently by the conservation movement.

The reasons people hunt with guns are many, but they are honest and civilised, not secretive or cruel. Nor is shooting used simply as an excuse to lay bets on a result.

The laws and traditional codes by which the sport is governed are adhered to by the majority of the participants.

Shooting is responsible for much of the British countryside's present richness and diversity, and it has a definite place in the future management and sustainable use of resources.

● The above is an extract from *Shooting – country sport and conservation*, a teachers' resource pack published by The British Association for Shooting & Conservation. See page 39 for address details.
© *The British Association for Shooting & Conservation*

The 'no hunting – no deer' argument

Information from the League Against Cruel Sports

Hunt propagandists claim that if deer hunting with hounds were abolished, it would lead to the extermination of the red deer of Exmoor and the Quantock Hills. They base this alarmist threat on the following suppositions.

1 'Farmers currently tolerate deer on their farms and suffer the consequent crop losses because the deer provide them with "sport" as a compensation. Without this incentive farmers would not tolerate deer on their land and would shoot the deer lawfully by day and unlawfully at night.'

A poll taken in the area of Exmoor in February 1985 by NOP Market Research Ltd found that only 17% of Exmoor residents approved of hunting deer with hounds. Of those involved in farming, 58% either opposed or had no view on hunting.

Much of the territory of the red deer on Exmoor and the Quantock Hills is owned by the National Parks Authority, the County and District Councils, the National Trust, the Forestry Commission, the League Against Cruel Sports and many private individuals sympathetic to deer. Therefore the minority of pro-hunt farmers who, in the event of a hunt ban, could be so intolerant of deer that they might try to destroy them simply do not own enough land to make an impact on deer numbers.

Even if a small number of farmers decided to go out of their way to kill deer, they could only legally do so during daylight. Licences from the Ministry of Agriculture, Fisheries and Food for the shooting of deer at night have been extremely difficult to obtain, and present MAFF policy is to refuse such licences. There are penalties for unlicensed night shooting of deer and it is unlikely that even the most embittered pro-hunting farmer would undertake such a risk.

The hunt supporters' argument is that hunting farmers do not shoot deer on their land as they wish to preserve them for hunting. This is not true as records from game-dealers in the south-west reveal that some hunting farmers also shoot deer and sell the venison.

Finally, hunters claim that hunting farmers are true conservationists. They conversely state that these 'conservationists' will exterminate Britain's largest living mammal and the very symbol of Exmoor National Park if hunting is prohibited. Both statements cannot be true.

2 'Without the vested interest of hunting farmers and landowners in deer, vigilance against poaching would cease with a consequent increase in poaching.'

The poaching of deer has always been present to some degree, whether within hunting territory or without; however, it is likely to become less of a problem as modern deer farming increases the legal availability of inexpensive venison – and therefore lessens the rewards for poaching. There is no evidence to show that poaching is any more or less of a problem in areas where deer are hunted than elsewhere.

It is not credible to suggest that the modern conservation-minded residents of Exmoor and the Quantock Hills would not remain vigilant against poaching if hunting was banned. The hunt's claim of being a force against poaching has been shown to be false by the recent convictions of deer-hunting supporters for the poaching of deer.

3 'Hunting causes deer to disperse across a wide area and therefore prevents intensive crop losses caused by large groups of deer.'

The opposite is true. The fact is that deer, like other herbivorous prey species, form larger groups when they are aware of predators. Packs of hounds pose the only obvious threat to deer, and this threat is the principal cause of large deer concentrations and consequent crop damage. It is noticeable that when the hunting season ends in April the large herds break up and disperse.

4 'It is not possible to shoot deer safely on Exmoor and in the Quantock Hills.'

The overwhelming majority of deer killed in Britain, both within and outside hunting territory, are shot humanely by rifles. The Exmoor herd requires an annual cull of some 1,000 deer – of which only about 50 to 100 are killed by hunting with hounds. Deer are controlled humanely and successfully by shooting in all areas of Britain – even in populated areas such as the New Forest where the deer are shot safely from 'high-seats' – the bullet being fired downwards so that it goes into the ground in the event of a miss.

The late David Stephen, well-respected naturalist, who had extensive experience of deer-culling in Scotland, wrote in *The Scotsman* in 1988: 'Down south you'll hear it said that the red deer on Exmoor and around about could not be culled in the Highland manner, that is with a rifle. This is nonsense which any Highland stalker would laugh out of existence. The Devon and Somerset Staghounds hunt in country with well-wooded valleys, and is tailor-made for shooting red deer from high seats as the Forestry Commission does with roe deer.'

5 *'During two periods when hunting ceased in the Exmoor area, the red deer were decimated.'*

The first period when hunting was suspended was in the mid-1600s when the Civil War led to royalty suspending its deer hunting in the area. In the absence of the monarch and his hunting parties, the impoverished local population took advantage of the absence of the threat of death, mutilation and deportation and killed deer for food.

The period 1824-1854 is the one most often quoted by hunt supporters as being a time when hunting with hounds did not occur – a cause, it is claimed, of deer being almost wiped out. However, G. Kenneth Whitehead in his book *Hunting and Stalking Deer* provides evidence that hunting continued for 20 of these 30 years

During this time when hunting was less regular, the deprived rural community again exploited a valuable and normally inaccessible source of food.

Today's communities are not the same half-starved, desperate communities of the 1600s and mid-1800s. Many residents have moved to the area to enjoy the aesthetic stimulation of wildlife and would not tolerate the extinction of the very symbol of Exmoor.

Deer exist all over Britain – red deer living in many other parts of the country including South Devon, Norfolk and Scotland without the spurious protection of hunting.

6 *'Deer thrive on Exmoor because of the existence of hunting with hounds. On neighbouring Dartmoor there are no deer because there is no hunt to protect them.'*

The red deer of Dartmoor were exterminated in the 1700s by the Duke of Bedford's Staghounds! This is an example of stag-hunting being responsible for the extermination of deer.

The Nature Conservancy Council (now English Nature) does nor consider deer hunting necessary for the preservation of deer. The Assistant Regional Officer of the NCC South-West Region wrote of deer hunting: 'We feel that this is a moral and animal welfare issue, not one of nature conservation.' (Ref: Letter dated 28 February 1989.)

7 *'Stag-hunting only continues due to its popularity and support in the farming community.'*

Many farmers and landowners have no choice but to tolerate hunting as they do not own the sporting rights. A proportion of the profit is diverted into a 'front company' controlled by senior officers of the hunt. The Badgworthy Land Company was established by hunt supporters to prevent the further loss of hunting territory. It continually seeks out landowning farmers in need of finance and has purchased thousands of acres of 'sporting rights' over the years. Thus whatever happens to the ownership of the land, the sporting rights remain in the hands of hunting interests, and landowners are unable to prohibit hunting on their land.

The NOP poll of 1985 showed that only 17% of Exmoor residents supported hunting, and that of those involved in farming 58% either opposed or had no views on the issue. It is clear therefore that even in its main remaining stronghold, the demise of deer hunting would be welcomed by more than would grieve it.

In the Quantocks, hunting is even more unpopular amongst the community than on Exmoor. The residents of the Quantock village of Holford have frequently complained about the Quantock Staghounds and have petitioned the National Trust to ban the hunt from its land around the village.

8 *'Hunting with hounds is a near-natural method of control.'*

Hunting with hounds is totally unnatural. Wild predators such as wolves select the old, sick and weak specimens of a herd of deer. If the animal can outrun the wolves for a few minutes, the predators give up. Their object is economy – a short chase and quick kill to provide food for the pack. Conversely the object of deer hunting is to provide a long chase for the subscribing followers. It is the task of a hunt servant known as a 'harbourer' to select a fit, strong, 'warrantable' deer for the hunt. Thus deer hunting is the opposite of natural selection. There is no natural predator in the world which hunts its quarry for 20 miles over a period of several hours – and which uses motor-cyclists equipped with CB radio to keep track of the running deer!

● The above is an extract from *Wildlife Protection – The case for the abolition of hunting and snaring*, published by the League Against Cruel Sports. See page 39 for address details.

© League Against Cruel Sports

Photo: League Against Cruel Sports

What is drag hunting?

Information from the League Against Cruel Sports (LACS)

In the time of the Stuart kings a popular sport was hound racing where the speed and scenting ability of a hound was tested by laying a trail over a certain distance and matching the hound against others. This was gradually adapted into drag hunting. In her book *Drag Hunting*, (J.A. Allen, 1978) Jane Kidd reveals that often when foxes could not be found, fox-hunts, completely unknown to the following riders, would get a whipper-in to dip the lash of his whip in aniseed and gallop off 'hallooing' across the country trailing his scented whip behind him. The hounds would pick up the line and the riders would follow until the whipper-in disappeared into a covert and claimed that the 'fox' had gone to ground. Jane Kidd wrote,

'This method of showing sport remained a closely guarded secret amongst hunt staff.'

This illustrates just how easy it is to change a fox-hunt into a drag hunt. The sport became very popular in colleges and the military. Jane Kidd explains,

'It was ideal for sporting youth – the impatient and brave who hunted to ride rather than rode to hunt.'

Oxford University was one of the first to form a drag hunt closely followed by Cambridge University. (Both packs still operate today.) The Household Brigade formed a drag hunt in 1863, the Royal Artillery at Woolwich in 1866 and the Staff College and Royal Military Academy in 1869.

The modern drag hunts were formed much later – for instance the North-East Cheshire in 1958, the Anglesey in 1973, the Berks & Bucks in 1974 and the Saddleworth (re-established) in 1985. They tended to arise in areas where motorways, housing and wire fences made much territory inaccessible and where fox-hunting had been reduced to a few gallops along tracks. Drag hunts also emerged where no foxes existed such as Jersey and the Isle of Man.

Jane Kidd wrote, 'Drag hunting is becoming an increasingly practical sport, not merely because of the encroachment of urbanisation on the countryside, but also because it demands little sacrifice on the part of the farmers.'

Drag hunts can be run to suit the character of their members. The cautious can form a chase with small obstacles and short lines. The fearless can join a drag hunt which builds huge fences and lines 15 miles long.

How does a drag hunt work?

To a casual observer and indeed to most riders, a drag hunt looks exactly like a fox-hunt. A huntsman and one or two whippers-in control the hounds as they follow the scent of their 'quarry', and are followed by riders galloping behind. As in fox-

Photo: League Against Cruel Sports

hunting there are followers too, chasing around in cars, on bicycles or on foot trying to get a view or seeking vantage points to watch hounds puzzling out the scent-line.

A rider, or perhaps a runner, will have set off some time before the hunt, perhaps half an hour, depending on the length of the line. This 'drag-man' will lay a scent trail by dragging a sack soaked in a liquid or perhaps squirting the scented liquid from a squeezy bottle as he rides or runs the chosen route.

The line will have been devised between the Master of the Hunt and local farmers so there is no danger of the hounds and riders disturbing livestock or crops, and avoiding main roads and railway lines. The 'drag-man' could take the line for around 4 miles. Then the drag will be lifted so that when the hounds reach the end of the line, the whole hunt can stop for a rest. Then they will be off again on another line. At the end of the hunt the hounds will be rewarded with food instead of tearing up a fox. There will have been no trespass as the 'drag-man' can choose safe places to take the scent. And of course no wild animals will have been chased and killed.

Some people have asked, '*But what if the hounds put-up a fox or deer? Won't they hunt and try to kill it?*'

Of course, experience shows that a pack of hounds may divert on to an animal which jumps up in front of them but in most cases the huntsman should be able to call them off. In the case of drag hounds putting up a red, fallow or roe deer, the hounds would have great difficulty in hunting it for long without the full encouragement of the huntsman and the assistance of a host of followers.

In the case of drag hounds 'rioting' after a fox, there will of course be no stopping up of fox earths and badger setts, as in fox-hunting. So the fox could escape down the nearest hole and be totally safe because a drag hunt has no need of terriers!

A further advantage of switching from fox-hunting to drag hunting relates to badgers. All over the country badgers would be relieved from the stress of being blocked into their setts by hunt 'earth-stoppers' and having to lose valuable winter foraging time digging themselves out at night when the hunt is over. Even when fox-hunters do not block up badger setts, hounds often chase foxes into setts and mill around the entrances.

The scent left by hounds and humans around the setts is known to cause badgers to delay emergence at night – again reducing valuable foraging time.

The League Against Cruel Sports has never heard of any incident where drag hounds or bloodhounds out hunting have caused any problems to wildlife, crops, livestock, pets or road and rail traffic.

Bloodhounds

In a bloodhound pack there are fewer dogs used than in a drag hunt. Instead of a rider or a runner dragging a scented bag, the hounds follow the scent of the runner himself, or the 'clean boot' as it is called. An athlete or team of athletes is used – again on a route predetermined for safety and with the agreement of farmers and landowners. When the bloodhounds catch their 'quarry', again they receive a food reward and much praise to ensure that next time they are keen to follow the scent.

Riding to bloodhounds is becoming enormously popular with half a dozen new 'hunts' being formed in the last decade.

● The above is from *Drag hunting – a family sport*, by the League Against Cruel Sports. See page 39 for address details.

© League Against Cruel Sports

BFSS *on drag hunting*

The British Field Sports Society replies to the findings of a recent League Against Cruel Sports NOP poll on drag hunting

1,000 farmers were surveyed. 52 per cent said that they allowed fox-hunting on their land. This is a very low figure and would not equate to the number of farmers in particular hunt country who allow the hunt. Some of the farmers surveyed would be in areas where there is no hunting at all, and others in areas which the hunt avoids because of unsuitability of terrain, proximity to motorways etc. The farmers who 'allowed' hunting tended to be on the larger farms. It must also be said that many farmers, if rung out of the blue about hunting, would be concerned that it might be 'the antis' and therefore some of the responses may not be genuine.

Of those farmers who currently allow fox-hunting on their land. 42 per cent said they would allow drag hunting. The League claims this means that every hunt could make the change and would have access to an area '300 times the size of St James' Park'. This offers no help to the anti-hunt case. Its own results have shown less than half of the farms which currently allow fox-hunting would

be available to draghunting. How many of these farms would be suitable for drag hunting is another question altogether.

Only 1 in 6 of those who do not 'allow' hunting (or who do not have a hunt in their areas to 'allow') would allow drag hunting. (Again, whether those farms would be suitable is unknown.)

Quite apart from the simple fact that drag hunting and fox-hunting are entirely different sports, it appears to us that this survey offers no support to the suggestion that drag hunting could (or should) replace fox-hunting. As drag hunts tend to maintain considerably fewer hounds and do not do deadstock collection, many jobs would still be lost. It is also debatable whether farmers who say they would welcome the drag hounds would do so if no deadstock collection service was being provided.

The League once again proves its total ignorance of all types of hunting. Hunting a drag or 'the clean boot' are totally different sports to fox-hunting, and they are purely for the cross-country rider. All those who

currently enjoy following hounds on foot would be excluded. The suggestion that ANY type of hunt could operate with access to farmland – '300 times the size of London's St James' Park' is ludicrous in the extreme – that's only 15,000 acres. Even a small fox-hunting country will cover over 100,000 acres and drag hunting requires a lot more open land.

The League's document is full of inaccuracies and false assumptions – even assuming that the poll gives as clear a picture of farmers' attitudes to hunting, which our own knowledge indicated is doubtful. Foxhound packs involve more hounds, more staff and more horses so even if all packs could change over there would still be job losses.

But the biggest losers would be the fox and countryside conservation. It is highly likely that more foxes would be killed for control purposes in the absence of fox-hunting and there would be no need to manage fox coverts in a way which benefits all wildlife.

© British Field Sports Society

INDEX

ADDITIONAL RESOURCES

You might like to contact the following organisations for further information. Due to the increasing cost of postage, many organisations cannot respond to enquiries unless they receive a stamped, addressed envelope.

Advocates for Animals
10 Queensferry Street
Edinburgh
EH2 4PG
Tel: 0131 225 6039
Protects animals from cruelty and prevent the infliction of suffering. Produces a wide range of booklets on animal experiments and animal sports.

Animal Aid
7 Castle Street
Tonbridge
Kent
TN9 1BH
Tel: 01732 364546
Opposed to any use of animals in medical research.

Biomedical Research Education Trust
58 Great Marlborough St
London
W1V 1DD
Tel: 0171 287 2595
Supports the responsible use of animals in medical research. Leaflets, factsheets, videos and speakers available.

British Association for Shooting & Conservation
Marford Mill
Rossett
Wrexham
LL12 0HL
Tel: 01244 573000
Fax: 01244 573001

British Diabetic Association
10 Queen Anne Street
London
W1M 0BD
Tel: 0171 323 1531

British Field Sports Society
59 Kennington Road
London
SE1 7PZ
Tel: 0171 928 4742
Fax: 0171 620 1401
Ensures the continuation of field sports. They publish books, videos, factsheets, posters, leaflets and a student resources pack. Able to provide speakers throughout the country.

British Union for the Abolition of Vivisection (BUAV)
16a Crane Close
London
N7 8LB
Tel: 0171 700 4888
Fax: 0171 700 0252
Strives for the total abolition of vivisection. Campaigns at local and national levels against vivisection. Provides information to the public and media including a wide range of factsheets and other publications.

Cosmetic Toiletry & Perfumery Association (CTPA)
Josaron House
5-7 John Princes Street
London
W1M 9HD
Tel: 0171 491 8891
Fax: 0171 493 8061
Represents the cosmetics companies.

FRAME
Russell & Burch House
96-98 North Sherwood Street
Nottingham
NG4 4EE
Tel: 0115 958 4740
Fax: 0115 950 3570
Promotes the concept of alternatives to animal experiments. Work towards reducing the number animals used, refining methods to reduce suffering and replacing live animal methods with reliable alternative techniques.

Humane Research Trust (HRT)
Brook House
29 Bramhall Lane South
Bramhall
Cheshire
SK7 2DN
Tel: 0161 439 8041
Fax: 0161 439 3713
Supports medical and scientific research by advanced techniques which replace the use of laboratory animals.

League Against Cruel Sports (LACS)
83-87 Union Street
London
SE1 1SG
Tel: 0171 403 6155
Campaigns for a change in the legislation to wildlife proper protection and outlaw hunting with dogs.

Research Defence Society (RDS)
58 Great Marlborough Street
London
W1V 1DD
Tel: 0171 287 2818
Supports the responsible use of animals in medical and biological research. Leaflets, factsheets, videos and speakers available.

Royal Society for the Prevention of Cruelty to Animals (RSPCA)
The Causeway
Horsham
West Sussex
RH12 1HG
Tel: 01403 264181
Fax: 01403 241048
Produces a wide range of leaflets and other materials on animal welfare issues. Please contact the Enquiries Service.

The St. Andrew Animal Fund
10 Queensferry Street
Edinburgh
EH2 4PG
Tel: 0131 225 2116
Fax: 0131 220 6377
Wants to reform the law and the administration of legislation, relating to the care and use of living animals in research experiments and for laboratory purposes.

ACKNOWLEDGEMENTS

The publisher is grateful for permission to reproduce the following material.

While every care has been taken to trace and acknowledge copyright, the publisher tenders its apology for any accidental infringement or where copyright has proved untraceable. The publisher would be pleased to come to a suitable arrangement in any such case with the rightful owner.

Chapter One: Animal Experiments

Is animal research justified?, © British Diabetic Association, October-December 1996, Campaigning to end animal experiments, © BUAV, Information about animal research, © Biomedical Education Trust, 1996, Why do we use animals for research?, ©Humane Research Trust, Vermin or life-saver, © Research Defence Society, Alternatives to animal experiments, © RSPCA, You don't have to dissect, © Animal Aid, 'Animal reearch helped save my daughter's life', © Research Defence Society, A few people in the UK who benefited last year from medical research involving animals, © Research Defence Society, Animals in research, © Advocates for Animals, The alternative to animal testing, © FRAME, Animal research and the devlopment of a new medicine, © The Association of the British Pharmaceutical Industry, Cosmetics and product testing, © Animal Aid, Animal testing – your questions answered, © Cosmetic, Toiletry & Perfumery Association Information Service, New products, © RSPCA.

Chapter Two: Blood Sports

What's wrong with animal rights?, © BFSS Communications Ltd, Hunting, © Animal Aid, Shooting sports – live quarry, © The British Association for Shooting & Conservation, Bloodsports in Britain, © The St Andrew Animal Fund, © This is fox-hunting, British Field Sports Society, The ethics of shooting, © The British Association for Shooting & Conservation, The 'no deer – no hunting' argument, © League Against Cruel Sports, What is drag hunting?, © League Against Cruel Sports, BFSS on draghunting, © British Field Sports Society.

Photographs and Illustrations

Pages 1, 5: Katherine Fleming / Folio Collective, pages 11, 14: Research Defence Society, pages 12, 19: Andrew Smith / Folio Smith, page 21: Animal Aid, pages 26, 35, 36: League Against Cruel Sports, page 29: The British Association for Shooting & Conservation.

Craig Donnellan
Cambridge
January, 1997